Now What?
The IRS is Taking
Everything I Own.
Help!

Can the IRS and Department of the Treasury really do that? You don't have to just watch as your bounty is hauled away, there are ways to navigate these nasty waters.

Jeffrey A. Schneider
EA, CTRS, NTPIF

ISBN: 978-0-578-40921-4

Published by: SFS Tax Problem Publishing
Edited by: Jeffrey Schneider, EA, CTRS, NTPIF
Design and composition by: Jeffrey Schneider, EA, CTRS, NTPIF
Cover design by: Angie Alaya

Issued also as an eBook.

Now What? The IRS is Taking Everything I Own. Help!

is also available in e-book.

For ordering information or special discounts for bulk purchases, please contact:

Visit: http://nowwhathelp.com or http://igotataxnotice.com for more information

Table of Contents

Life Saving Navigation

DEDICATION

This book is dedicated to several people, four of whom are no longer with me. Firstly, my parents, Seymore and Lillian Schneider. My Dad passed away in 1992 and he never saw me in private practice. It was he who got me into preparing taxes as he prepared taxes for many years before his illness. Mom passed away unexpectedly in 2007 just as I was negotiating the opening of my second office at the time of her passing. I hope they are both proud of what I have been able to achieve.

Then there is my baby sister, Lauren Fried, who passed in March 2018. She was not a well person but was always encouraging me in whatever I did.

And Ali's Mom, Ilene Kirsch. She lived with us for over 10 years until she passed away in 2012. She was with us when I opened both of my offices. Mom was as happy for us as we were.

I miss them all dearly, and I wish they could see me, now, with two offices, our daughter working with us and two published books.

This book is also dedicated to Ali's Dad, Bob Kirsch. Thankfully, Bob, at age 91, is still very much among the living, and is healthy and active. He is always there with a joke, but most of all with his love and support. Thank you, Dad.

To my children, Marissa and Cameron Adler. For over 18 years, you allowed me to be a part of your life. Hopefully, I was able to help you, along with Mom, to become the outstanding adults that you are today. I am so proud of who you have become. Thank you, "chickens."

And, of course, to my business partner, best friend, and wife, Ali. Like all married couples, we have had our share of trials and tribulations but we have muddled through them all and persevered.

As I mentioned in the first book, she began bugging me to begin the second book just as soon as the first one was published. Now that the second book is completed, she is pestering me for a third book. Ali, if it were not for you, we would not be where we are today.

ACKNOWLEDGEMENT

Thank you to all of my teachers, fellow presenters, and instructors who gave up their valuable time to share their knowledge with me throughout the years.

Thank you to my Enrolled Agent family around the country (and some were my teachers or instructors) for giving of yourself and passing along your wisdom.

To Larry Lawler and the staff of the American Society of Tax Problem Solvers (ASTPS), to Attorney Extraordinaire, Steve Klitzner and to the members of the Rozbruch Mastermind Group of 2017 - 2019, thank you for your support, encouragement, suggestions and constructive (though sometimes harsh) criticism as you help me and SFS Tax Problem Solutions continue to grow.

FOREWORD

You are guilty until proven innocent.

Wait. What? That sounds backward, right? After all this is the United States of America. Everyone knows you are innocent until proven guilty. Perhaps in a court of law, but when it comes to the IRS, you are deemed guilty until you can prove otherwise.

When the IRS determines you owe them money, they don't have to wait long to collect. They can, and often do, immediately and aggressively begin collections. I know this because for 16 years I owned and operated an IRS representation firm helping individuals and small businesses that were in trouble with the IRS. We negotiated settlements on their behalf, settling legitimate tax debt for a fraction of what was owed, and we did penalty abatements, getting our clients' money back after the IRS had assessed erroneous or excessive penalties.

Four and half years ago, I exited that business to teach other tax professionals how to successfully do what I did. One of my first students was Jeffrey A. Schneider, the author of this book. I'd like to say I taught him everything he knows, but that wouldn't be true. While I've had years of experience coaching him with his practice, as an Enrolled Agent, Jeff is federally licensed to represent clients before the IRS. He's also a Certified Tax Resolution Specialist and a Fellow of the National Tax Practice Institute. But credentials tell only part of Jeff's story. Jeff was already someone practitioners listen to, he is a sought-after expert who travels across the country to teach the technical aspects of tax representation to other Enrolled Agents, tax attorneys, and CPAs. He knows how to represent clients better than anyone, and he does it because he cares about people.

Jeff and I share a passion for tax resolution work, and this passion is rooted in our sincere desire to help people whose lives are being turned upside down by the IRS. In this book, Jeff explains your rights as a taxpayer, and you have many. He will tell you what to do if the IRS has placed a lien on or has seized money from your bank account, is garnishing your wages, and/or is withholding part or all of your tax refund to offset state taxes due, back child support or unpaid student loans. Remember, with the IRS, you are guilty until you prove yourself innocent, and they can and will make you pay unless you get the help you need to stop them from taking your money.

This book can help you get your life back. It is truly an indescribable feeling to go to bat for a client and help solve his or her tax problem. You're just one person, going up against the IRS, in a fight for your financial life. The IRS is the most brutal collection agency on the planet, with unbridled power to enforce the country's tax laws. It's David versus Goliath, and you are going to need help to win.

This book is a good beginning. Jeff knows what you're going through. He has fought this fight for taxpayers just like you. Dealing with the IRS is complicated. The average taxpayer doesn't have a clear understanding of the tax laws, and they don't know how to defend their rights. They don't know how to navigate the IRS maze. Jeff does. Jeff uses clear, down-to-earth language that will help you make a plan to get your money, and your life, back. What better person to listen to other than the person other licensed professionals listen to?

Michael Rozbruch, CPA,
Certified Tax Resolution Specialist (CTRS)

AUTHOR'S NOTE

What?
Taxes, what a dry and droll topic. However, it is a
subject that is never going to go away,
no matter what members of Congress
(on either side of the aisle) want!

"...but in this world nothing can be said to be certain, except death and taxes."

— **Benjamin Franklin**

"This is a question too difficult for a mathematician. It should be asked of a philosopher."

— **Albert Einstein** (when asked about completing his income tax form)

"A penny saved is worth two pennies earned . . . after taxes."

— **Randy Thurman** (a certified financial planner and CPA)

Never were truer words spoken. I have written this book to explain and dissect certain situations when your money can be taken by the U.S. Government, whether it's by the Internal Revenue Service or by special federal agencies, and what rights they have to do that. Most importantly, we talk about what recourse you have to prevent that from happening.

Most people know that refunds can be commandeered when you owe back taxes, but did you know that the U.S. government can also take these refunds when there are other debts owed?

This book will discuss what those are. What happens when one spouse does something underhanded, whether it be during or before the marriage? Does the innocent or injured spouse have any recourse? This book discusses that too.

It will not tell you everything that can be done, nor does it provide all the procedures and rules that you must adhere to. That would make this book longer than *War and Peace*. However, it does provide guidance as to what can happen.

I do mention throughout this guide that professional help, from an Enrolled Agent (like yours truly), a Certified Public Accountant, or an attorney, may be warranted.

So, dear reader, if you find yourself in any of the situations that are in this book, you should think about enlisting professional help so that a stressful situation isn't any more stressful than it needs to be. Allow an experienced captain who's navigated these treacherous waters many times before guide you. There is help out there!

INTRODUCTION

Getting Your Sea Legs

This book is the second in a series that is meant to guide tax professionals and taxpayers through the process of what happens when the IRS starts taking what is yours.

My first book, *Now What? I Got a Notice from the IRS, Help!* is available via Amazon, on Kindle, and has just been released as an audio book. This book may not help the non-professional in dealing directly with the Internal Revenue Service. You should contact an experienced tax professional, such as an Enrolled Agent, Certified Public Accountant, or an Attorney when dealing with the IRS… (more on that later), but it should help you demystify what happens when the IRS or any other government agency wants to take what is yours.

In this tome, I will explain why the IRS will take a tax return's refund, withdraw cash from your bank account, garnish your wages, social security benefits, and pensions, and seize your property, as well as what you can do about it. I will also discuss how the government will take these items for other past debts, such as owing child support or defaulting on a student loan. As you can imagine, this is a very scary thought.

The Internal Revenue Service is the world's largest and most aggressive collection agency on the planet, and they will use whatever authority they have to get what they are entitled to.

To make matters worse, other federal or state government agencies will enlist the help of the IRS to get what they are entitled to. The IRS can just swoop in and take your stuff and go to your employer, your vendors, and your clients as well as your bank to fork over whatever you have in order to pay them (and potentially others) what you owe. While it may not be that simple, you get the idea.

In this book, I will also describe the various Federal Tax Offset and U.S. Department of Treasury Offset programs. I hope to explain your options in combating these aggressive tactics. I have been in the field of taxation for four decades and I have seen a lot, good and bad, when it comes to dealing with the IRS.

So, stay tuned and hold onto your bank accounts and
paychecks for dear life,
for the seas are rough and the ride is going to be a bit
bumpy.

CHAPTER 1

You Owe Taxes, Now What?

Now Who Is Captain Jeffrey A. Schneider and How is He Qualified to Navigate the Murky Tax Seas? What is an EA, CTRS, NTPIF?

I am an Enrolled Agent, or EA. As I will discuss in more detail later, an EA is the only federally licensed tax professional. I have been helping taxpayers like you file tax returns, respond to IRS notices, and solve their IRS debts for over 35 years. I have an undergraduate degree in finance and a master's degree in taxation. I worked for a time in corporate America, in addition to working various positions in private practice in different tax departments, culminating in a tax director position for a major jewelry retailer/wholesaler.

> *An EA is the only federally licensed tax professional.*

My practice, consisting of tax return preparation and taxpayer representation, is physically located on Florida's Treasure Coast, with a satellite office in Palm Beach. This beautiful area lies on the southeastern coast of Florida and I have clients all over the country.

In 2010, I became a fellow of the National Tax Practice Institute, a 72 credit-hour program provided by the National Association of Enrolled Agents (NAEA). This program focuses solely on the many facets of representing taxpayers, individuals, and businesses before the IRS. In 2015, I passed an advanced exam offered by the American Society of Tax Problem Solvers (ASTPS) to become a Certified Tax Resolution Specialist (CTRS). I recently obtained the ACT – E, Advanced Crypto Tax Expert designation.

Over the years, I have given back to the profession through leadership at the local, state, and national levels. I have been president of two local chapters of the Florida Society of Enrolled Agents (FSEA), was elected president of the FSEA in 2013, and held the title of Director of the National Association of Enrolled Agents (NAEA).

I was also a founding and five-year member of the NAEA's Educating America Task Force, whose primary mission is to promote the EA credential and help individuals to prepare or want to prepare tax returns take the next step and become Enrolled Agents.

I also give many presentations on tax matters to other organizations and local governments.

After leaving New York in 1987 (and then Atlanta in 1990), I moved to Florida and have resided in the Sunshine state for the past 27 years. I live as a pseudo-empty nester in Port St. Lucie with my wife, Ali, and our "four-legged son," Boodah.

Most recently, I had the honor of being selected to serve a three-year term on the Internal Revenue Service Advisory Council, or IRSAC. The purpose of IRSAC as a whole and its various subgroups is to make recommendations to the Internal Revenue Service to ensure a fair and just tax system for all. I was chosen to be on the Office of Professional Responsibility (OPR) Subgroup. The OPR department's vision, mission, strategic goals, and objectives support effective tax administration by ensuring all tax practitioners, tax preparers, and other third parties in the tax system adhere to professional standards and follow the law.

OPR's goals include the following:

1. Increase awareness and understanding of Circular 230 and the OPR through outreach activities,

2. Apply the principles of due process to the investigation, analysis, enforcement, and litigation of Circular 230 cases and

3. Build, train, and motivate a cohesive OPR team.

The job of the subgroup is to make recommendations to help OPR achieve their goals.

CHAPTER 2

The Name of the Game, or How the IRS Deals with Mutiny on the High Seas

We live in a "volunteer" tax society. Now, what does that actually mean? Many believe that this means they can voluntarily file returns and pay taxes. We call these people tax protestors.

Tax protestors do not file and pay taxes for a variety of reasons. Rest assured, they never win, not only when dealing directly with the Internal Revenue Service, but also when they take the IRS to court

So, again, what does voluntary mean? As you know, we are required to file and pay our "fair share" of taxes (whatever that definition is). If we do not, just like the tax protestors, we will get into all sorts of trouble. The voluntary part is that we voluntarily put the numbers on the return. Many countries in the civilized world "create" a return for their citizens, or their citizens just report their income and the country's taxing agency "bills" them for the tax due. As you should know, if you have to file a return here in the U.S., you must report all of your income (as all income is reportable, unless it is not), and you report the applicable tax deductions. Then, you compute the tax and pay it to the IRS.

Again, what does this mean to all Americans? I am sure that you have heard of a "little" book called the Internal Revenue Code. Not including the 1,100 pages of the Tax Cuts and Jobs Act that was passed in December 2017, there are 74,608 pages in the federal tax code (though this includes many repealed statutes) according to a 2016 *Washington Post* article. In addition, there are almost 10,000 actual sections in the code.

Not only that, but the federal tax code is 187 times longer than it was a century ago, according to Commerce Clearing House, a well-known publisher of tax and accounting materials which has analyzed the code since 1913. Amazingly, during the first 26 years of the federal income tax's existence, the tax code only grew from 400 to 504 pages. Even through President Franklin Roosevelt's New Deal, the tax code stayed well under 1,000 pages. Changes made during World War II caused the tax code to balloon to 8,200 pages. However, most of the growth came in the past 30 years, from 26,300 pages of tax code in 1984 to nearly three times that length today. When you add another 6,400 pages of Internal Revenue Service regulations (IRS interpretations and clarifications), that is a lot of law. If you are interested in a history of the Internal Revenue Code, check   out https://en.wikipedia.org/wiki/Internal_Revenue_Code .

Which system do you like best? I tend to like ours, but I am biased. As the Toby Keith song goes, "I am proud to be an American," and I take the good with the bad. But I digress… let's get back on point.

Toward the beginning of the Code, there is a very important Section, §61, which states that "all income, from whatever source it is derived, is taxable." This means that, if you earn money, be it from working, a business, earning interest, realizing dividends, under the table, etc., is reportable and, in most cases, taxable. However, along the way, located in these many pages of tax code, there are exclusions, exemptions, and exclusions to the exclusions that may render some items not taxable.

The Internal Revenue Code does not require taxpayers to claim deductions, exemptions, or even credits. You do not have to list your dependents, take mortgage interest (if you can itemize your deductions, though you have to deduct the standard deduction based on your filing status), or even claim married filing jointly, even if you are, indeed, married (you must file married filing separately in that case). You also do not have to claim credits such as the dependent care credit or the child tax credit. All that is required for you to do is to report your income, your one exemption (or two if filing jointly), and the standard deduction. It must be noted that the exemption deduction was eliminated by the Tax Cuts and Jobs Act of 2017.

As you may have guessed, I have just provided you with a definition of what "voluntary" means when it comes to tax compliance.

As an aside, all of this information has to be reported on forms designed by the Commissioner of Internal Revenue. And just who and what is the commissioner? The Commissioner is the head of the Internal Revenue Service and reports directly to the Secretary of the Department of the Treasury, though various Congressional committees and subcommittees require the Commissioner to answer for his actions and the actions of his direct and indirect reports. His, and there have only been two female Commissioners in the history of the IRS, Shirley D. Peterson and Margaret Milner Richardson, as well as one Acting Commissioner, Linda E. Stiff, duties include administering, managing, conducting, directing, and supervising "the execution and application of the internal revenue laws or related statutes and tax conventions to which the United States is a party." He also advises the President on the appointment and removal of a Chief Counsel of the IRS. The Commissioner reports to the Secretary of the Treasury through the Deputy Secretary of the Treasury.

Upon the resignation of John Koskinen, David J. Koulter served as "acting" Internal Revenue Service Commissioner. In January, President Donald J. Trump nominated California Tax Attorney, Charles "Chuck" Retting to serve as the new commissioner for the next several years. Mr. Retting was approved by the Senate on September 12, 2018, and was sworn in on October 1, 2018, for a term to expire on November 12, 2022. He will oversee an agency that deals with $3.4 trillion (that's right, trillion with a "T") in revenues. And if you are wondering, "Why not Koulter?," understand that he holds another important position with the IRS, which he was also performing while serving as Commissioner. He will continue on as the Assistant Secretary of the United States Treasury for Tax Policy.

So, what about reporting income and expenses? As required, we have to report all income and all applicable and legal deductions, which could just be the standard deduction, then compute a tax. If you had federal income taxes withheld (and not social security (FICA) and Medicare taxes), or you had a credit from a prior period, or made estimated tax payments, you may be entitled to a refund of your own money.

If you owe? Well, that is where many people get themselves into trouble.

Many taxpayers keep their withholdings low, make small estimated tax payments or, heaven forbid, do not make any. The rationale is that they need the money to pay for their everyday lives. They will make arrangements with the Internal Revenue Service, they think.

Sure, the IRS will gladly allow for a payment plan under their Fresh Start Program. However, you have to pay a certain amount per month based on their criteria and numbers.

What happens if you cannot pay what the IRS wants? Many try to ignore the notices (you should read my first book, which demystifies many of the notices that the IRS sends).

Like the Glenn Close character in the movie Fatal Attraction, the IRS does not like to be ignored. And if you do ignore them, the IRS will start taking your assets, from cash, to property, cars, etc.

You can thank the Federal Offset Program for this power.

However, owing taxes is not all that falls under this program. We will address more of what can be "offset" (i.e., taken, seized, etc.) as we progress through this book.

You may have heard, unless you have been living in a bomb shelter, that Congress passed, and President Trump signed into law, the largest tax reform since 1986.

An almost complete rewrite of the Internal Revenue Code, the Tax Cuts and Jobs Act was signed into law on December 22, 2017.

Considering how all the politicians pledged "tax simplification," this new law has so many complicated parts that makes the term tax simplification seem like an oxymoron. In fact, many of the provisions sunset (expire) in 2025.

To give you an idea how wide-reaching this law is, the executive summary is 86 pages. As I type this, the IRS has just issued more regulations and FAQs, at 184 and 14 pages alone, respectively. However, in the year I am writing this book, we will be having mid-term elections, and if the ruling party changes in either or both houses, all bets are off. We could even have a Tax Increase Act of 2018. Wouldn't that be fun, boys and girls?

The Tax Cuts & Jobs Act, as I stated before, was enacted as a revision of the last set of tax laws in 1986, which revised the Code of 1954. I remember the '54 Code as I have been in this field almost 40 years…before 1986 was even on the hazy horizon.

In addition, you may remember that when the government shut down in mid-January 2018, Congress finally agreed to a three-week reprieve. Then, on February 9, 2018, Congress passed a bi-partisan budget plan which funded the government for the rest of the fiscal year, which ends on September 30 of each year (prior to 1976, it ended on June 30). In addition to funding the government so it could be kept running at "full-strength," it also extended 75 provisions of the previous law that had expired on December 31.

So, what is the big deal, you may ask? First, they extended these provisions retroactively to January 1, 2017. Examples of these formerly expired tax provisions are: the tax deduction for mortgage insurance premiums, tuition fee deduction, and credits for the purchase of certain hybrid or electric vehicles. The most important one is the ability to exclude the cancellation of debt of the mortgage on your principal residence (under Internal Revenue Code §108). If this code section was not extended, taxpayers who could not claim an exemption, like in a bankruptcy, had to pay tax on the income that is now taxable like all other cancellation of debt (i.e., credit card or car loan debts).

Many taxpayers, and you may be one of them, may prefer to get their tax returns prepared and filed early and out of the way, especially if a refund is expected. If you are one of the millions who filed early because you had no reason to know that Congress would extend certain parts of the law that you were now able to take advantage of, you had to amend you return. And if you were like the many, many taxpayers who have a tax professional (such as an Enrolled Agent or CPA) prepare your return, you probably had to incur additional costs in order to do so. On top of that, amended returns cannot be electronically filed (at least in 2018, they could not) and refunds from amended returns, in general, take longer to process than electronically transmitted returns.

An amended return, for those not in the know, is just what it sounds like. It is a return that reflects changes, up or down, to income – a deduction not reflected in the original return, as long as it is filed before the various statutes of limitations. Generally, a claim for a refund has to be made within three years from the due date of the return.

There is another option, called a "superseded" return. This is when you correct a return and file it before its original due date (i.e., April 15). This type of return, when marked as "superseded" across the top of page one of Form 1040, Individual Tax Return, cancels the original return. It's as if the original was never filed. Trust me, dear readers, this is a much better option.

CHAPTER 3

You Have It, We Want It

Forget 10,000 Leagues Under the Sea.
You'll have to dive much deeper than that to get to the
heart of the IRS.

It is a behemoth of a bureaucracy, with levels upon levels, and just when you think you have arrived at its core, you find many more levels underneath all of those.

In the administration and enforcement of our tax system, there are four basic levels: Examinations (commonly known as Audits), Collections, Appeals and Criminal Investigations (CID). I will not discuss CID here as I will presume, that although mistakes happen and items get missed, we are not dealing with fraud and criminal intent.

When a return is filed and the IRS processes it (whether it be paper or electronic), it is deemed self-assessed. It is also deemed correct and all is right with the world, unless the IRS computers find a discrepancy, or you get audited and the auditor or Revenue Agent finds errors or omissions. An audit, by the way, can be performed locally or via the mail (this is called a "correspondence audit").

If the computers find an error, you'll get a notice called a CP 2000, which is part of the IRS underreporting program. This is a notice which basically says that "you reported this, but the IRS has that."

What type of errors are picked up by the computers?

Well, the Internal Revenue Service receives various information returns, just like you do. If you understate the income as reported on these forms (i.e., W-2 income, 1099s for rental income, interest and dividend income) or overreport expenses (i.e.,1098s for mortgage interest or mortgage insurance premiums), or report that you had health insurance when you, in fact, did not (Form 1095), the computer spits out a notice showing you what they have versus what you have reported on your return.

You have the right to dispute the claim in whole or in part. You will then pay the tax on none, all, or some of what the IRS says you owe (as well as interest and possibly penalties). In an audit, the IRS will send you an audit report, which says that you owe tax, and possibly interest and penalties as well. If you agree with any of these, the amount owed is entered on your IRS tax account. If you do not pay right away, the bills start to arrive, or worse.

If you disagree what was stated in the CP 2000, you can send in documentation to dispute it. Just like in a regular, in-person audit, the correspondence audit will ask for documentation on one or several items that were reported on your return. Generally, it does not cover everything on your return as an in-person audit might. Correspondence audits are becoming more and more common as the IRS funding keeps getting cut with each Congressional budget.

What causes issues with taxpayers, other than when a taxpayer gets an audit notice and they do not have documentation for the expenses they claimed, is the fact that they underreported their income.

Some taxpayers believe that if they do not get a form, say a 1099-MISC, they do not have to report the income. Or, if they get cash, they do not have to report that, either. Many believe that no form equals no reporting and no tax. I hope that you all know that this is a big fat lie.

Let me give you a hypothetical. If you are a residential service provider (i.e., house cleaner, landscaper, or pool servicer), you get paid by the homeowner and they will never send you a 1099. Let us further assume that that you get $100 per month for 12 months from 1,000 homeowners. Besides being a nice business, it equates to a gross annual revenue of $1,200,000. I hope you aren't thinking about not reporting this income. Even if it is all cash, and even if you do not put it in the bank, you must report it. Even if you have a loss, meaning you have more than $1,200,000 in expenses, you still must report all of your income.

If you recall, I mentioned the statute of limitations (SOL). One SOL that I did not mention (in fact, I only mentioned one of the several related to taxes), is the six-year statute. If you underreport income by 25%, the IRS has six years to audit you, double the standard audit period of three years.

> *If you underreport your income too much, it can be*
> *deemed fraud and there is no SOL on fraud.*
> *In other words, the IRS can audit you forever.*

Even in a commercial scenario, where you perform services for a business (i.e., commercial cleaning, computer repair, etc.) and you earn $590 for the year, you must still report it as income even if they pay you in cash and you don't deposit it into a bank account. Let us also assume that this happens for 1,000 customers, and for your other customers, you make more than $600. Now, if you have customers that pay you over $600, they will/should send you a 1099-MISC. All the others will not, as the rule for sending out 1099s is when a business pays another business/individual over $600 in any one year for services rendered. Again, I hope you are not considering not reporting the cash revenue in your gross revenue numbers (that is $590,000, or $1,000 x $590) just because you did not get a 1099.

Now, what happens if all your 100 clients paid you $700 for the year? You received only 998 1099's because, let's say, you moved to a new space, the forwarding stopped, and you did not provide two customers your new address. Maybe you did one job for each of these businesses, and it was during early January. You received cash and, as with a lot of things, "out of sight, out of mind." Both customers, plus the other 998, sent the IRS a 1099 and one to you, too, as required. However, for one reason or another it was never forwarded to you (or worse yet, you lost it). Will you report only $698,000 ($700 x 998)? The IRS should have received a thousand Forms 1099s in your name and social security (or Federal ID) number. As such, reporting only $698,000, and not the full $700,000, will generate a CP 2000. Missing $2,000 is not so bad.

And if you did not get any 1099s (or maybe you did and just forgot all the cash you received) and you never reported the $70,000, the CP 2000 will compute the tax and add interest and penalties (which could be up to 25% of the taxes owed, if, that is, they deem there was no fraud). This could amount to a lot of money.

Please do not get the impression from my two examples that I am advocating not reporting all of your income, depending on the amount. On the contrary, what I am saying is that "You earn it, you report it."

Now, let's discuss collections. The Internal Revenue Service is the world's largest and most aggressive collection agency on the planet. Even with their funding woes, they can and will come after you, be it in person or via a letter. They have also resorted to contracting with outside collection agencies for long-overdue debt. If you owe more than $51,000, they also work with the various states to prevent you from renewing or applying for a passport.

One of the IRS collection units is the Automated Collections Service, or ACS. These men and women are located in various service centers around the country. They are primarily Revenue Officers (RO), which represent a higher level in the pecking order than do the Revenue Agents (RA), (the IRS employees who conduct field or office audits). These Revenue Officers are also located in the field, housed in local IRS offices. Though most communications are conducted by letter, they can also make "house calls" to the taxpayer's home or business in order to collect a tax debt.

Generally, Revenue Officers are better trained and educated than Agents, not to say that Agents are not educated. Many are CPAs, and I have known a few that are attorneys. They tend not to become EAs until after they leave the IRS, as achieving this designation is automatic once they are in this position for five years and submit their application. Unlike "normal" folks, these individuals do not have to take the Special Enrollment Exam to become an Enrolled Agent.

The next group of employees are called Settlement Officers (SO). These officials are usually in the IRS Appeals Office, where taxpayers who disagree with an RO's or RA's findings can appeal, or request that a fresh pair of eyes look over the documents and review the arguments on both sides of the coin. These appeals can spring from a disagreement with IRS findings in an in-person audit, a correspondence audit, or even from a CP 2000. It can also happen when the taxpayer applies for a collection alternative (an offer in compromise or an installment agreement) and does not agree with the decision. The right to appeal is one of the rights included in the Taxpayer Bill of Rights. (The full Taxpayer Bill of Rights is provided later in this book).

The caveat when dealing with appeals is that they tend not to look at new issues (de novo). They will, however, review new evidence to justify the claims made by the taxpayer which disputes the findings of the Revenue Agent or the Revenue Officer.

A taxpayer usually gets one shot at appeals, which has far-reaching authority. The next step (as long as procedures are followed) is to prepare and file a tax court petition. Generally, you can file this once you get what is commonly known as the 90-day notice (Statutory Notice of Deficiency). This notice gives you 90 calendar days to file a petition. You also have the right to file a petition when you get a notice of determination that is a rejection of your claim by an Appeals Officer. You can prepare the petition yourself or by a U.S. Tax Court Practitioner (a very special designation that non-attorneys can achieve by taking an exam which has the distinction of having a very low passing rate), or by an attorney licensed to practice in your state. You will pay the fee (currently $60) and then wait until your petition gets on the court docket and receives a docket number. It is then assigned to an IRS lawyer. It must be stated that most of the time when you file a U.S. Tax Court (USTC) petition, the IRS attorneys will "send it back to appeals," as most cases are not USTC worthy (i.e., not enough money).

If do not want to go to court (it is not cheap unless you do it yourself, and that is not highly recommended) and you cannot and do not pay (i.e., ignore IRS letters), that is the crux of this book. Stay tuned!

Just as you have the right to appeal an IRS decision, you also have the right to be represented. As in a criminal or civil action, you do not have to navigate the waters alone. A USTCP or licensed attorney can prepare a tax court petition and represent you in the

U.S. Tax Court. Only a licensed attorney can represent you in other courts (i.e., the U.S. District Court, the U.S. Circuit Court, the Federal Court of Claims and, of course, the U.S. Supreme Court).

CHAPTER 4

The Taxpayer Representative: There's More to Sailing than Leaving the Dock

Not everyone is qualified to be a captain of a ship. When you're miles from land and things get dicey, you want an Admiral, not a weekend sailor. You need a professional who knows what he or she is doing.

Up to that point when/if your case gets remanded back to appeals, there are other two credentialed professionals that can represent you: the Certified Public Accountant and the Enrolled Agent.

I have to say that I am quite biased and prejudiced in certain parts of this section. I also have a personal stake in my opinions and how I state the facts, all of which are 100% true. However, for full disclosure, I am an Enrolled Agent, one of America's Tax Experts®. I am very proud of this designation and I take the requirements to achieve it and maintain it very seriously.

I strongly believe that I owe it to my readers and to the taxpaying community to explain in detail exactly who are legitimate taxpayer representatives and who may be trying to pass themselves off as legitimate taxpayer representatives.

I am not talking about individual companies. Instead, I am going to discuss the credentials, as only individuals can achieve these credentials, not to mention prepare a tax return. I do not care who these individuals work for, but I have to say, let the buyer beware of some of these large companies that perform taxpayer resolution work. There are some good ones out there, but also many, many bad ones.

First, outside of a convicted felon, anyone can prepare a tax return for money.

Actually, even a felon can prepare a tax return, but he or she cannot sign it, as it is illegal.

Generally, anyone who prepares (or assists in preparing) a federal tax return for money must have a Preparer Tax Identification Number (PTIN). They must sign in the paid preparer's area of the return (see Exhibit No. 1) and give the taxpayer a copy of the return.

Exhibit No 1

Third Party Designee	Do you want to allow another person to discuss this return with the IRS (see instructions)? ☐ Yes. Complete below. ☐ No			
	Designee's name ▶	Phone no. ▶	Personal identification number (PIN) ▶	☐☐☐☐☐
Sign Here	Under penalties of perjury, I declare that I have examined this return and, to the best of my knowledge and belief, it is true, correct, and accurately lists all amounts and sources of income I received during the tax year. Declaration of preparer (other than the taxpayer) is based on all information of which the preparer has any knowledge.			
Joint return? See instructions.	Your signature	Date	Your occupation	Daytime phone number
Keep a copy for your records.	Spouse's signature. If a joint return, **both** must sign.	Date	Spouse's occupation	If the IRS sent you an Identity Protection PIN, enter it here (see inst.) ☐☐☐☐☐☐
Paid Preparer Use Only	Print/Type preparer's name	Preparer's signature	Date	Check ☐ if self-employed PTIN
	Firm's name ▶		Firm's EIN ▶	
	Firm's address ▶		Phone no.	

Most tax return preparers provide outstanding service, however, they have differing levels of skill, as well as continuing education requirements and expertise. Another important difference is their ability to represent taxpayers before the Internal Revenue Service.

Representation rights fall into two categories: *unlimited* and *limited* representation.

Preparers with *unlimited* representation rights

- can represent their clients on any matters, including audits, payment collection issues, and appeals.

Those with *limited* representation rights

- can only represent clients whose returns they have prepared and signed, and only before revenue agents, customer service representatives, and similar IRS employees, including the Taxpayer Advocate Service.

Credentialed Return Preparers

Tax return preparers with **unlimited** representation rights include professionals with the following:

- **Enrolled Agents** - Enrolled Agents are licensed by the IRS. They are subject to a suitability check and must pass a three-part Special Enrollment Examination (SEE), a comprehensive exam that requires them to demonstrate proficiency in federal tax planning, individual and business tax return preparation, and representation. They must complete 72 hours of continuing education every three years. Enrolled Agents may represent any taxpayer in any tax matter before all administrative levels of the IRS. All enrolled agents must also have a valid PTIN.

- **Attorneys** – Licensed by state courts, the District of Columbia, or their designees (such as the state bar), attorneys have earned a degree in law and passed a bar exam. Attorneys generally have ongoing continuing education and professional character standards. Attorneys may offer a range of services; some attorneys specialize in tax preparation and planning.

- **Certified Public Accountants** – Licensed by state boards of accountancy, the District of Columbia, and the U.S. territories, CPAs have passed the Uniform CPA Examination. They have completed a study in accounting at a college or university and have also met the experience and good character requirements established by their respective boards of accountancy. In addition, CPAs must comply with ethical requirements and complete specified levels of continuing education in order to maintain an active CPA license. CPAs may offer a range of services; some CPAs specialize in tax preparation and planning.

Annual Filing Season and the Registered Tax Return Preparer Programs

Though the IRS recognizes the efforts of non-credentialed return preparers who aspire to a higher level of professionalism, this is not a credential. A few years before the writing of this book, the IRS attempted to regulate all tax preparers that are not Enrolled Agents (they already do that), CPAs, or attorneys. To that end, they created a new category, one with limited rights. They called this the Registered Tax Return Preparer, or RTRP. The program began in March 2012 and ended with a final District Court decision. Why did it end? You will have to wait as I first explain what the case was about.

The IRS tried to not only regulate all tax preparers to protect the taxpayer community, they also wanted to make sure that all had some level of minimum competency.

As with all individuals who want to prepare any return, these individuals had to:

- Get a PTIN.

- Complete 15 credits of continuing education, consisting of:

  - 10 hours of federal tax law,

  - three hours of tax law updates,

  - and two hours of ethics, every year.

- Take an annual competency test. The IRS administered this test, just as they do the SEE.

36

However, there were tax preparers who felt that the IRS did not have the right to **require** them to take continuing education or show minimum competency by taking a test. They sued in court, won, sued in appeals, and won again. They did not argue the real reason for the lawsuit (in my humble opinion, taking continuing education or showing minimum competency), but based their case on the fact that the IRS did not have the legal authority to regulate tax preparers *at all*. They could regulate who *represents* taxpayers before them (EAs, CPAs, and attorneys), but not preparers. The final appeal came down in 2013 when the IRS decided not to take this issue to the U.S. Supreme Court.

In January 2013, the IRS issued the following announcement:

"On Jan. 18, 2013, the United States District Court for the District of Columbia has ordered the Internal Revenue Service to stop enforcing the requirements for registered tax return preparers. In accordance with this order, tax return preparers covered by this program are not currently required to register with the IRS, to complete competency testing or secure continuing education. The ruling does not affect the regulatory practice requirements for CPAs, attorneys, enrolled agents, enrolled retirement plan agents or enrolled actuaries.

IRS filed an appeal and it lost its case, heard on September 24, 2013, and a decision to cease this program was handed down on February 11, 2014."

I did not go into the case details here, but if you are interested in learning more, check out Sabina Loving, et al. vs. Internal Revenue Service, et al., heard in the District Court for the District of Columbia

Why didn't the IRS take away all representation rights, even limited rights, unless you were an EA, a CPA or an attorney? I do not really know. However, that is a conundrum that we have to deal with. My point in telling you all this is that, if any tax preparer tells you that s/he is a RTRP, they are not being truthful. In fact, the IRS issued an order instructing preparers to stop using that acronym or designation. However, they are also not enforcing it.

In light of the loss in Loving, the IRS created a volunteer program, the *Annual Filing Season Program*. With this program, tax preparers who obtain 18 hours of continuing education for a specific tax year, including a six-hour federal tax law refresher course with a test, receive an *Annual Filing Season Program Record of Completion*. <u>Like the RTRP, this is not a credential or a license.</u> To be honest, I am not sure what it is. As I said, it is strictly voluntary and does not apply to Enrolled Agents, as they have already taken a test (the SEE) and their own education to continue to be an Enrolled Agent. Since CPAs and attorneys are regulated by the state in which they live/work, they do not have to follow this program.

Just as with those in the RTRP program, tax return preparers who participate in the Annual Filing Season Program have limited representation rights and may only represent clients whose returns they prepared and signed, and only before revenue agents, customer service representatives and similar IRS employees, including the Taxpayer Advocate Service. They must participate in the Annual Filing Season Program in both the year of return preparation and in the year of representation. Again, they cannot represent clients whose returns they did not prepare. They also cannot represent clients regarding appeals or collection issues, even if they did prepare the return in question.

Non-credentialed return preparers who do not participate in the Annual Filing Season Program may prepare and file federal tax returns, but they cannot represent clients before the IRS even if they prepared the return. This is a big step forward.

Tax Professionals with Specialized Credentials - Are You Adrift in Alphabet Soup?

Just for your edification: In addition to attorneys, CPAs, and Enrolled Agents, the IRS recognizes the credentials of two other types of specialized tax professionals who are included in the Directory of Federal Tax Return Preparers. They include:

- **Enrolled Actuary** - Enrolled actuaries have satisfied the standards and qualifications as set forth in the regulations of the Joint Board for the Enrollment of Actuaries and have been approved by the Joint Board to perform actuarial services required under the Employee Retirement Income Security Act of 1974.

- **Enrolled Retirement Plan Agent** - Enrolled retirement plan agents (ERPAs) are licensed by the IRS and specifically trained in certain retirement plan matters. ERPAs are subject to a suitability check and must pass a two-part ERPA Special Enrollment Examination. They must also complete 72 hours of continuing education every three years. ERPAs may represent clients before the IRS on certain retirement plan matters.

The point that I am trying to make here is this: If you receive a notice and are dealing with an audit, you cannot just walk into any tax return preparer's office. Only an Enrolled Agent, a CPA, or an attorney can help you with any IRS issue.

I have mentioned Enrolled Agents, Certified Public Accountants, and attorneys throughout this section. What is the real difference?

- All Enrolled Agents who practice as Enrolled Agents are tax professionals. Some may only prepare returns, some may only represent clients in collections and/or audits, and some may do both.

- CPAs and attorneys are not necessarily tax professionals. I have many attorney clients as well as CPAs who refer work to me because they do not delve into tax or representation. They just prepare tax returns.

What is the SEE? It is a three-part exam that is 100% tax and ethics.

- Part 1 focuses on individual taxation, covering income from various sources, deductions, and credits, as well as specialized items such as estate and gift tax. It also touches upon an EA's advisory role. Here is what is included in this portion of the test:

  - Preliminary Work and Taxpayer Data

  - Income and Assets

  - Deductions and Credits

  - Taxation and Advice

- Specialized Returns for Individuals

- Part 2 covers business taxation. Here is what is included in this portion of the test:

  - Business Entities

  - Business Financial Information

  - Specialized Returns and Taxpayers

- Part 3 contains IRS procedures and practice issues. Here is what is included in this portion of the test:

  - Practices and Procedures

  - Representation Before the IRS

  - Specific Types of Representation

  - Completion of the Filing Process

You can visit this website to see more detail on what the test includes: (https://ipasseaexam.com/irs-see-exam-format/).

Additionally, only Enrolled Agents are required to take 100% of their education on tax (which includes two hours of ethics). CPAs and attorneys take courses every year, which may happen to include many tax topics. However, they are not required to take any on tax. Most of the education for their license is in accounting and auditing, and tax is not a part of either one of those subjects. They are also licensed in the state in which they passed the exam, unless their state has reciprocity with another. I know several attorneys and CPAs that have licenses in multiple jurisdictions.

EA licenses are issued and regulated by the Internal Revenue Service by virtue of its Return Preparer's Office. However, it is the Office of Professional Responsibility (OPR) that is our watchdog. They oversee all individuals who prepare tax returns and have a PTIN, as well as EAs, CPAs, and attorneys when they represent clients before the IRS. We must also follow a set of rules called Circular 230, which was updated in 2014.

In January 2018, I had the distinct honor of being selected to serve a three-year term on the Internal Revenue Advisory Council's OPR subgroup.

The CPA must have, as stated above, a college degree that is 150 college credits. In addition, they need to earn a certain number of graduate program credits. Some states allow for work experience in lieu of some college hours.

They must also take an exam called the Uniform CPA Examination, which is issued in 55 jurisdictions. Each jurisdiction has their own set of requirements that must be met in order to sit for the exam as well as to maintain their license. The CPA Exam is developed, maintained, and scored by the American Institute of Certified Public Accountants (AICPA) and administered in partnership with the National Association of State Boards of Accountancy (NASBA).

Like the SEE, this exam is electronic and given at Prometric sites around the country. Since 2004, it has had four parts, consisting of:

- Auditing and Attestation
- Financial Accounting and Reporting

- Regulations (which includes tax)

- Business Environment and Concepts

There is an expression that the CPA initials stand for something other than Certified Public Accountant...it stands for "Can't Pass Again." This is such a notoriously hard exam that all who have passed it deserve kudos.

When is a Set of Initials Not a Professional License?

There are many strings of initials floating out there, put out on the blue waters by many organizations.

There are the National Association of Enrolled Agents (NAEA), the American Institute of Certified Public Accountants (AICPA), the American Society of Tax Problem Solvers (ASTPS), the America Institute of Certified Tax Coaches (AICTC) and Commerce Clearing House (CCH), a publisher, to name a few.

Whatever they are offering requires studying and some testing. However, you must realize, these are not licenses.

In the field of tax preparation and taxpayer representation, there are only three licenses, and they are the EA, the CPA, and an attorney. Make sure you choose the right captain before you step on the ship. It is critical when attempting to navigate the deep, dark waters of the IRS.

In the spirt of full disclosure, in addition to becoming an Enrolled Agent, I have achieved three additional sets of initials: a CTRS,

NTPI Graduate Fellow, and an ACT-E. Allow me to explain these designations.

- The NAEA offers a program where one takes 72 hours of courses over three 24-hour units, all related to taxpayer representation (not tax return preparation) through their National Tax Practice Institute (NTPI). The program is only offered to licensed individuals, meaning that only EAs, CPAs, or attorneys can take this program. Upon completion, the professional becomes a Fellow of NTPI. This designation shows dedication to professional education and competence.

- I am also a Certified Tax Resolution Specialist (CTRS), which is offered by the ASTPS (American Society of Tax Problem Solvers). I took a 100-question exam, which included a case to solve, and was kissing the blessed shoreline once I passed this difficult exam. Individuals who become a CTRS are demonstrating their dedication to their craft.

- I recently obtained the ACT – E, Advanced Crypto Tax Expert designation. This designation was earned after taking 44 classes and passing a test after each session. It shows that I have the knowledge to help taxpayers that are involved in the world of crypto or virtual currency.

I am sharing this information with you so that you are aware that not all credentials are created equal. When interviewing potential tax professionals with initials after their names other than the ones covered here, be sure to ask about them.

Ask what those initials mean in the big scheme toward solving your problem. After all, you'll be on the boat together and entrusting him or her with your financial life.
You deserve to be certain you have the right one before you turn over the controls.

The CTRS is a specific designation for solving tax resolution issues, like the ones we will talk about in this book. The same goes for the NTPI fellowship. All other initials relate to many different things, some dealing with tax, some not. There are also different requirements for earning different credentials. You should also ask as to the number of continuing education credits they take, for example.

The bottom line is this: Don't be shy about asking the questions you need to ask to get the full picture when you compare professionals and their accomplishments.

Researching Tax Return Preparers Before You Climb on Board

The IRS has a searchable, sortable public directory at https://irs.treasury.gov/rpo/rpo.jsf to search for various tax return preparers. This directory contains only those with a valid PTIN who hold a professional credential or who have obtained an Annual Filing Season Program Record of Completion from the IRS.

The IRS Directory of Federal Tax Return Preparers with Credentials and Select Qualifications contains the name, city, state, and zip code of credentialed preparers and Annual Filing Season

Program participants. Taxpayers can also research the type of credentials or qualifications held by specific tax professionals. It is important to note that the listings do not serve as an endorsement by the IRS.

Other Players Who Will You Encounter in the Deep Blue Ocean

In addition to the Internal Revenue Service, there are other government agencies that have a hand in what we are discussing.

One is the U.S. Treasury Investigator General for Tax Administrations, or TIGTA. TIGTA's tag line, as shown on www.treasury.gov, is "Promoting Integrity in the Administration of Internal Revenue Laws." The agency was established in 1998 to "provide independent oversight of the IRS."

TIGTA makes sure that the IRS performs its duties as required by law and follows its own policies (Internal Revenue Manual, or IRM) and does not cross the line, especially when dealing with taxpayers and their representatives.

As an example, a few years before this book's publication, there was an issue with regards to applications by organizations to be considered "not-for-profit," or tax-exempt, organizations. Congress ordered TIGTA to investigate... and investigate they did. They did find irregularities in the processes as well as in the approval process (or lack of approval, in this case). In fact, many high-level IRS personnel were fired or reassigned. Former

Commissioner Koskinen came under direct fire for this issue, which was partially responsible for his resignation.

In my opinion, probably the most important "quasi-government/IRS agency" is the Office of the National Tax Advocate, currently headed by Nina Olson. This independent department of the Internal Revenue Service was established on July 30, 1996, two years before TIGTA, as a result of the Congress passing the Taxpayer Bill of Rights 2. The Taxpayer Advocate Service, or TAS, assists taxpayers and their representatives in dealing with the IRS when there is hardship or administrative or systemic problems that do not seem to be getting resolved at the Agency level (exam, appeals, or collections). Each state has at least one case advocate. There are 1,400 case advocates and 1,800 employees overall that make up the TAS.

As I mentioned, the Office of the National Tax Advocate (NTA), is currently headed by Nina Olson. She is located in Washington, DC. Her title is the National Taxpayer Advocate...yes, that's right, just like the office she heads. She is the only Internal Revenue Service employee authorized to make legislative suggestions directly to Congress, which she does twice a year. These reports, which are available to the public though the NTA site at https://taxpayeradvocate.irs.gov/reports, identify the top problems and issues taxpayers and tax professionals face when dealing with the Internal Revenue Service. As Ms. Olson has said, "I am truly an independent voice inside the IRS," as no one sees her reports before they are presented to Congress – not even her boss, the Commissioner of Internal Revenue.

Although the Taxpayer's Bill of Rights 2 was where the Office of the National Tax Advocate got its start, it replaced the Office of the Ombudsman (now part of the Department of State). It was not until 2015, after Ms. Olson repeatedly suggested that a new comprehensive Taxpayer Bill of Rights (TIBOR) be enacted, that this bill of rights came to be, due to her efforts (more on this in the next section).

CHAPTER 5

The Protection and Fundamental Rights You have with the IRS

We all know that the Thomas Jefferson wrote the United States Bill of Rights. But did you know that as a taxpayer, you have your own Bill of Rights? As such, the IRS has adopted a Taxpayer Bill of Rights as proposed by National Taxpayer Advocate, Nina Olson.

The Taxpayer Bill of Rights applies to all taxpayers in their dealings with the IRS. It groups the existing rights in the tax code into ten fundamental rights, and makes them clear, understandable, and accessible.

These 10 rights hold the IRS to certain standards, just like they hold taxpayers and their representatives to specific standards. The TIBOR is embedded in Internal Revenue Code §7803(a)(3), which is the section that holds the Internal Revenue Service responsible for their actions.

1. The Right to Be Informed

Taxpayers have the right to know what they need to do to comply with tax laws. They are entitled to clear explanations of the law and IRS procedures in all tax forms, instructions, publications, notices, and correspondence. They have the right to be informed of IRS decisions about their tax accounts and to receive clear explanations of the outcomes.

What This Means for You

If you receive a notice which fully or partially disallows your refund claim, the notice must explain the specific reasons why the claim is being disallowed.

- Generally, if you owe a penalty, each written notice regarding it must provide an explanation of it, including:

  - the name of the penalty,

  - the authority to assess the penalty given under the Internal Revenue Code,

  - and how the penalty is calculated.

- During an in-person interview with the IRS as part of an audit, the IRS employee must explain the audit process and your rights under that process. Likewise, during an in-person interview with the IRS concerning the collection of your tax, the IRS employee must explain the collection process and your rights under that process. Generally, the IRS uses Publication 1, *Your Rights as a Taxpayer*, as a guideline in meeting this requirement.

- The IRS must include, on certain notices, the amount (if any) of the tax, the interest, the penalties you owe, and an explanation of why you owe these amounts.

- The IRS must inform you in certain publications and instructions that when you file a joint income tax return with your spouse, both of you are responsible for all tax due and any additional amounts found to be due.

- The IRS must inform you in Publication 1, Your Rights as a Taxpayer, as well as in all collection-related notices that, in certain circumstances, you may be relieved of all or part of the tax owed on your joint return. This is sometimes referred to as "innocent spouse relief."

- The IRS must also explain in Publication 1, *Your Rights as a Taxpayer*, how it selects which taxpayers will be audited.

- If the IRS proposes to assess a tax against you, they will send you a letter providing the examination report which states the proposed changes. They will also provide you with the opportunity for a review by an Appeals Officer if you respond, generally within 30 days. This letter, which in some cases is the first communication from the examiner, must provide an explanation of the entire process, from examination (audit) through collections, and explain that the Taxpayer Advocate Service may be able to assist you. Generally, Publication 3498, *The Examination Process*, or Publication 3498-A, *The Examination Process (Audits by Mail)*, is included with this letter.

- If you enter into a payment plan (also known as an installment agreement), the IRS must send you an annual statement that states how much you owed at the beginning of the year, how much you paid during the year, and how much your remaining balance is.

- You have the right to access certain IRS records, including instructions and manuals issued to staff, unless such records are required or permitted to be withheld under the Internal Revenue Code, the Freedom of Information Act, or the Privacy Act. Certain IRS records must be available to you electronically.

- If the IRS is proposing to adjust the amount of tax you owe, you will typically be sent a Statutory Notice of Deficiency, which informs you of the proposed change. This notice provides you with a right to challenge the proposed adjustment in Tax Court without first paying the proposed adjustment. To exercise this right, you must file a petition with the Tax Court within 90 days of the date of the notice being sent (or 150 days if the taxpayer's address on the notice is outside the United States, or if the taxpayer is out of the country at the time the notice is mailed). Thus, the Statutory Notice of Deficiency is your ticket to Tax Court.

- The IRS should ensure that its written guidance and correspondence is accessible, consistent, written in plain language, and easy to understand.

2. The Right to Quality Service

Taxpayers have the right to receive prompt, courteous, and professional assistance in their dealings with the IRS, to be spoken to in a way they can easily understand, to receive clear and easily understandable communications from the IRS, and to have a way to file complaints about inadequate service.

What This Means for You

- The IRS must include information about your right to Taxpayer Advocate Service (TAS) assistance, and how to contact TAS, in all notices of deficiency.

- When collecting tax, the IRS should treat you with courtesy. Generally, the IRS should only contact you between 8 a.m. and 9 p.m. The IRS should not contact you at your place of employment if the IRS knows, or has reason to know, that your employer does not allow such contacts.

- If you are an individual taxpayer eligible for Low Income Taxpayer Clinic (LITC) assistance (generally your income is at or below 250% of the federal poverty level), the IRS may provide information to you about your eligibility for assistance from an LITC.

- For more information, see IRS Publication 4134, *Low Income Taxpayer Clinic List,* or find an LITC near you.

- Certain notices written by the IRS must contain the name, phone number, and identifying number of the IRS employee. All notices must include a telephone number that the taxpayer may contact. During a phone call or an in-person interview, the IRS employee must provide you with his or her name and ID number.

- The IRS is required to publish the local address and phone number of IRS offices in local phone books.

3. The Right to Pay No More than the Correct Amount of Tax

Taxpayers have the right to pay only the amount of tax legally due and to have the IRS apply all tax payments properly.

What This Means for You

- If you believe you have overpaid your taxes, you can file a refund claim asking for the money back, within certain time limits.

- You may request that any amount owed be removed if it exceeds the correct amount due under the law, if the IRS has assessed it after the period allowed by law, or if the assessment was done in error or violation of the law.

- You may request that the IRS remove any interest from your account that was caused by the IRS's unreasonable errors or delays. For example, if the IRS delays issuing a statutory notice of deficiency because the assigned employee was away for several months attending training, and interest accrues during this time, the IRS may abate this interest as a result of the delay. *IRC § 6404(e)*

- If you have a legitimate doubt that you owe part or all of the tax debt, you can submit a settlement offer, called an Offer in Compromise (Doubt as to Liability) on Form 656-L.

- You will receive an annual notice from the IRS stating the amount of the tax due, which will help you check that all payments you made were received and correctly applied.

- If you enter into a payment plan (also known as an installment agreement), the IRS must send you an annual statement that states how much you owe at the beginning of the year, how much you paid during the year, and your year-end balance.

4. The Right to Challenge the IRS's Position and Be Heard

Taxpayers have the right to raise objections and provide additional documentation in response to formal IRS actions or proposed actions, to expect that the IRS will consider their timely objections and documentation promptly and fairly, and to receive a response if the IRS does not agree with their position.

What This Means for You

- If the IRS notifies you that your tax return has a math or clerical error, you have 60 days to tell the IRS that you disagree. You should provide photocopies of any records that may help correct the error. In addition, you may call the number listed on your notice or bill for help. If the IRS agrees with your position, they will make the necessary adjustment to your account and send you a corrected notice.

- If the IRS does not adopt your position, it will send a notice proposing a tax adjustment (known as a statutory notice of deficiency). The statutory notice of deficiency gives you the right to challenge the proposed adjustment in the United States

Tax Court before paying it. To do this, you need to file a petition within 90 days of the date of the notice (150 days if the notice is addressed to you outside the United States). For more information about the United States Tax Court, see the Court's taxpayer information page.

- If you submit documentation or raise objections during a return examination (or audit), and the IRS does not agree with your position, it will issue you a statutory notice of deficiency. This notice will explain why the IRS is increasing your tax, which gives you the right to petition the U.S. Tax Court prior to paying the tax.

- When the IRS notifies you of plans to levy your bank account or other property, you'll generally have an opportunity to request a hearing before the Office of Appeals. Also, you'll generally have an opportunity to appeal the proposed or actual filing of a notice of federal tax lien.

5. The Right to Appeal an IRS Decision in an Independent Forum

Taxpayers are entitled to a fair and impartial administrative appeal of most IRS decisions, including many penalties, and have the right to receive a written response regarding the Office of Appeals' decision. Taxpayers generally have the right to take their cases to court.

What This Means for You

- The Commissioner must ensure an independent IRS Office of Appeals, separate from the IRS Office that initially reviewed your case. Generally, Appeals cannot discuss a case with the IRS unless you or your representative is given the opportunity to be present.

- The IRS must ensure that an appeals officer is regularly available within each state.

- If you do not agree with the proposed adjustment as a result of an examination (audit), you have the right to an administrative appeal.

- In certain situations, a taxpayer has the opportunity to request a conference with the Office of Appeals.

- You have the right to request an independent review conducted by the Office of Appeals prior to the termination of your installment agreement.

- If the IRS is proposing to adjust the amount of tax you owe, you will typically be sent a Statutory Notice of Deficiency, which informs you of the proposed change. This notice also informs you of your right to challenge the proposed adjustment in Tax Court without first paying the proposed adjustment. Thus, the statutory notice of deficiency is your ticket to Tax Court.

- To exercise your right to challenge the proposed adjustment in Tax Court *without* first paying the proposed adjustment, you must file a petition with the Tax Court within 90 days of the date of the notice being sent (or 150 days if the taxpayer's address on the notice is outside the United States, or if the taxpayer is out of the country at the time the notice is mailed).

- Under certain circumstances, the Office of Appeals has the exclusive authority to settle your case. Generally, for the four months after you petition the Tax Court, Appeals will be the only office within the IRS that can settle your case, as long as the Statutory Notice of Deficiency or other notice of determination was not issued by Appeals.

- Generally, you are entitled to request a Collection Due Process hearing to dispute the first proposed levy action relating to a particular tax liability. The independent IRS Appeals/Settlement Officer conducting your hearing must have no prior involvement with the taxes the IRS is attempting to collect. If you disagree with the hearing officer's determination, you can challenge it in Tax Court.

- If the IRS rejects your request for an offer in compromise (which asks the IRS to settle your tax debt for less than the amount owed) or for a payment plan (called an installment agreement), then you may seek an independent review of the rejection by the IRS Office of Appeals.

- You can generally request that an issue you have not been able to resolve with the IRS examination or collection division be transferred to the Office of Appeals. For issues that are unresolved after working with Appeals, you may request non-binding mediation (where a neutral third party will help you try to reach a settlement) or binding arbitration (where you and the IRS will be bound by a third party's decision). You may also request non-binding mediation or arbitration after unsuccessfully trying to enter into a closing agreement or offer in compromise.

- Generally, if you have fully paid the tax, and your tax refund claim is denied or if no action is taken on the claim within six months, then you may file a refund suit in a United States District Court or the United States Court of Federal Claims.

- In very limited circumstances, you can ask the court to make a determination on certain tax issues prior to an actual dispute between you and the IRS. For example, a court may be able to determine whether an organization is tax-exempt or if a retirement plan is valid.

- A jeopardy levy or assessment allows the IRS, in very limited circumstances, to bypass normal administrative safeguards and protections. For example, the IRS may issue a jeopardy levy if the IRS has knowledge that you are fleeing the country. If the IRS makes such a jeopardy levy or assessment, you have the right to file a lawsuit, and the court will determine whether the levy or assessment was reasonable under the circumstances as well as whether the amount is appropriate.

6. The Right to Finality

Taxpayers have the right to know the maximum amount of time they have to challenge the IRS's position, as well as the maximum amount of time the IRS has to audit a particular tax year or collect a tax debt. Taxpayers have the right to know when the IRS has finished an audit.

What this means for you

- The IRS generally has three years from the date you file your return to assess any additional tax for that tax year. There are some limited exceptions to this rule. For example, if you fail to file a return, or you file a false or fraudulent return, the IRS has an unlimited amount of time to assess tax for that tax year.

- The IRS generally has 10 years from the assessment date to collect unpaid taxes from you. The IRS can't extend this 10-year period unless you agree to extend the period as part of an installment agreement to pay your tax debt, or the IRS obtains a court judgment. However, there are some situations where the IRS may suspend the ten-year collection period and resume it later. The IRS may be able to do this if there's a period when the IRS cannot collect, such as times of bankruptcy or a collection due process proceeding.

- If you believe you have overpaid your taxes, you can file a refund claim asking for the money back. Generally, you must file a refund claim within three years from the date you filed your original return, or two years from the date you paid the tax, whichever is later.

- If the IRS sends you a notice proposing additional tax (statutory notice of deficiency), the notice must include the deadline for when you can file a petition with the Tax Court to challenge the amount proposed.

- To timely challenge a statutory notice of deficiency in Tax Court, you must file your petition within 90 days of the date of the statutory notice (150 days if the taxpayer's address on the notice is outside the United States or if the taxpayer is out of the country at the time the notice is mailed). If you do not timely file a petition, the IRS will assess the amount proposed in the statutory notice and you will receive a bill.

- Generally, the IRS can only examine (audit) your tax return once for any given tax year. However, the IRS may reopen a previously examined return if they find it necessary. For example, if there is evidence of fraud, the IRS can reopen an exam.

7. The Right to Privacy

Taxpayers have the right to expect that any IRS inquiry, examination, or enforcement action will comply with the law, be no more intrusive than necessary, and will respect all due process rights, including search and seizure protections and a collection due process hearing where applicable.

What This Means for You

- During a collection due process hearing, an independent IRS Appeals/Settlement Officer must consider whether the IRS's lien filing balances the government's need for the efficient collection of taxes with your legitimate concern that the IRS's collection actions are no more intrusive than necessary.

- The IRS cannot levy any of your personal property in the following situations: before it sends you a notice of demand, while you have a request for a payment plan pending, and if the IRS will not recover any money from seizing and selling your property.

- The IRS cannot seize certain personal items, such as necessary schoolbooks, clothing, undelivered mail, certain amounts of furniture and household items, and tools of a trade.

- There are limits on the amount of wages that the IRS can levy (seize) in order to collect tax that you owe. A portion of wages equivalent to the standard deduction combined with any deductions for personal exemptions is protected from levy.

- The IRS cannot seize your personal residence, including a residence used as a principal residence by your spouse, former spouse, or minor child, without first getting court approval, and it must show there is no reasonable alternative for collecting the tax debt from you.

- The revenue officer must attempt to personally contact you, and if you indicate the seizure would cause a hardship, he or she must assist you in contacting the Taxpayer Advocate Service if not providing the requested relief.

- The IRS issued interim guidance that extends these protections to suits to foreclose a lien on a principal residence. According to this guidance, the IRS should not pursue a suit to foreclose a lien on your principal residence unless it has considered hardship issues and there are no reasonable administrative remedies.

- As soon as practicable after seizure, the IRS must provide written notice to the owner of the property that the property will be put up for sale. Before the sale of the property, the IRS shall determine a minimum bid price. Before the property is sold, if the owner of the property pays the amount of the tax liability plus the expenses associated with the seizure, the IRS will return the property to the owner. Within 180 days after the sale, any person having an interest in the property may redeem the property sold by paying the amount the purchaser paid plus interest.

- If the IRS sells your property, you will receive a breakdown of how the money received from the sale of your property was applied to your tax debt.

- Under § 3421 of the Restructuring and Reform Act of 1998, IRS employees are required, "where appropriate," to seek approval by a supervisor prior to filing a Notice of Federal Tax Lien. Section 3421 further requires that disciplinary actions be taken when such approval is not obtained.

- The IRS should not seek intrusive and extraneous information about your lifestyle during an audit if there is no reasonable indication that you have unreported income.

- If you submit an offer to settle your tax debt, and the offer relates only to how much you owe (known as a Doubt as to Liability Offer in Compromise), you do not need to submit any financial documentation.

8. The Right to Confidentiality

Taxpayers have the right to expect that any information they provide to the IRS will not be disclosed unless authorized by the taxpayer or by law. Taxpayers have the right to expect the IRS to investigate and take appropriate action against its employees, return preparers, and others who wrongfully use or disclose taxpayer return information.

What This Means for You

- In general, the IRS may not disclose your tax information to third parties unless you give it permission, *e.g.*, you request that your professional disclose information in connection with a mortgage or student loan application.

- If a tax return preparer discloses or uses your tax information for any purpose other than for tax preparation, the preparer may be subject to civil penalties. If the disclosure or improper use is done knowingly or recklessly, the preparer may also be subject to criminal fines and imprisonment.

- Communications between you and an attorney with respect to legal advice the attorney gives you are generally privileged. A similar privilege applies to tax advice you receive from an individual who is authorized to practice before the IRS (*e.g.*, Certified Public Accountant, Enrolled Agent, and enrolled actuary), but only to the extent that the communication between you and that individual would be privileged if it had been between you and an attorney. For example, communication between you and an individual authorized to practice before the IRS regarding the preparation of a tax return is not privileged because there would be no similar privilege between a taxpayer and an attorney. The privilege relating to taxpayer communications with an individual authorized to practice before the IRS only applies in the context of noncriminal tax matters before the IRS, and noncriminal tax proceedings in a federal court where the United States is a party.

- In general, the IRS cannot contact third parties, *e.g.*, your employer, neighbors, or bank, to obtain information about adjusting or collecting your tax liability, unless it provides you with reasonable notice in advance. Subject to some exceptions, the IRS is required to periodically provide you a list of the third-party contacts upon request.

- The National Taxpayer Advocate and Local Taxpayer Advocates may decide whether to share with the IRS any information you (or your representative) provide them regarding your tax matter, including the fact that you've contacted the Taxpayer Advocate Service.

9. The Right to Retain Representation

Taxpayers have the right to retain an authorized representative of their choice to represent them in their dealings with the IRS. Taxpayers have the right to be told that, if they cannot afford to hire a representative, they may be eligible for assistance from a Low-Income Taxpayer Clinic.

What This Means for You

- If you have won your case in court, under certain conditions, you may be entitled to recover certain reasonable administrative and litigation costs related to your dispute with the IRS.

- In most situations, the IRS must suspend an interview if you request to consult with a representative, such as an attorney, CPA, or Enrolled Agent.

- You may select a person, such as an attorney, CPA, or Enrolled Agent to represent you in an interview with the IRS. The IRS cannot require that you attend with your representative, unless it formally summons you to appear.

- If you are an individual taxpayer eligible for Low Income Taxpayer Clinic (LITC) assistance (generally your income must be at or below 250 percent of the federal poverty level), you may ask an LITC to represent you (for free or a minimal fee) in your tax dispute before the IRS or federal court.

10. The Right to a Fair and Just Tax System

Taxpayers have the right to expect the tax system to consider facts and circumstances that might affect their underlying liabilities, ability to pay, or ability to provide information in a timely matter. Taxpayers have the right to receive assistance from the Taxpayer Advocate Service if they are experiencing financial difficulty or if the IRS has not resolved their tax issues properly and in a timely manner through its normal channels.

What This Means for You

- If you cannot pay your tax debt in full and you meet certain conditions, you can enter into a payment plan with the IRS where you pay a set amount over time, generally on a monthly basis.

- You may request that any amount owed be eliminated if it exceeds the correct amount due under the law, if the IRS has assessed it after the period allowed by law, or if the assessment was done in error or in violation of the law.

- You may request that the IRS remove any interest from your account that was caused by the IRS's unreasonable errors or delays. For example, if the IRS delays issuing a statutory notice of deficiency because the assigned employee was away for several months attending training, and interest accrues during this time, the IRS may abate the interest as a result of the delay.

- The time limit for asking for the taxes you overpaid to be refunded may be suspended during the time you are unable to manage your financial affairs due to a mental or physical health problem.

- If you have acted with reasonable care, you may be entitled to relief from certain penalties. Additionally, if you have a reasonable basis for taking a particular tax position, such as a claim for a refund, you may be entitled to relief from certain penalties. Reliance on the advice of a tax professional can, in certain circumstances, represent reasonable cause for the abatement of certain penalties.

- If you use a return preparer who takes an unreasonable or reckless position that results in underreporting your tax, that preparer may be subject to penalties.

- You can submit an offer in compromise asking the IRS to settle your tax debt for less than the full amount if you believe that: (1) you do not owe all or part of the tax debt, (2) if you are unable to pay all of the tax debt within the time permitted by law to collect, or (3) there are factors such as equity, hardship, or public policy that you think the IRS should consider in determining whether to compromise your liability.

- If you are experiencing a significant hardship because of an IRS action or inaction, you may be eligible for assistance from the Taxpayer Advocate Service (TAS). A significant hardship occurs when a tax problem causes you financial difficulties or you have been unable to resolve your problem through normal IRS channels. You may also be eligible if you believe an IRS system or procedure isn't working as it should. *IRC § 7803(c)*

- You have the right to request that the Taxpayer Advocate Service issue a Taxpayer Assistance Order (TAO) on your behalf if you are experiencing a significant hardship. TAS can issue a TAO ordering the IRS to take certain actions, cease certain actions, or refrain from taking certain actions. It can also order the IRS to reconsider, escalate to a higher level, or speed up an action.

- If you are trying to settle your tax debt with an offer in compromise based on your inability to pay, the IRS considers your income, assets, and expenses in deciding whether to accept your offer. Generally, the IRS uses guidelines for standard allowances to determine cost of living expenses, unless you will not be able to pay your basic living expenses. In that case, the IRS must consider your actual expenses. If you are offering to settle because you believe you don't owe the tax liability, you will not need to submit financial information.

- If you are a low-income taxpayer trying to settle your tax debt with an offer in compromise, the IRS cannot reject your offer solely on the basis of the amount of the offer. For example, it cannot reject an offer solely because the amount offered is so low it does not cover the IRS costs for processing it.

- If you submit an offer to settle your tax debt, and the offer relates only to how much you owe (known as a Doubt as to Liability Offer in Compromise), the IRS cannot reject your offer solely because it cannot locate your tax return to verify how much you owe.

- The IRS cannot levy (seize) all of your wages to collect your unpaid tax. A portion will be exempt from levy so that you can pay your basic living expenses.

- The IRS must release all or part of a levy and notify the person upon whom the levy was made if one of the following situations exist (1) the underlying liability is satisfied or becomes unenforceable due to the lapse of time, (2) the taxpayer enters into an installment agreement (unless the agreement specifies otherwise), (3) the release of the levy will facilitate collection of liability, (4) the IRS determines the levy is creating an economic hardship for the taxpayer, or (5) the fair market value of the property levied is greater than the liability, and releasing the levy on part of the property would not impair collection of the underlying liability.

- If you are an individual taxpayer eligible for Low Income Taxpayer Clinic (LITC) assistance (generally your income must be at or below 250 percent of the federal poverty level guidelines), you have the right to seek assistance from an LITC to ensure that your particular facts and circumstances are being considered by the IRS. A Statutory Notice of Deficiency is your ticket to Tax Court.

CHAPTER 6

The Internal Revenue Service Has a Right to Their Interests, and Yours as Well

Budget cuts or not, the IRS holds all the winning cards here. First, they can conclude that there is a debt, plus penalties and interest, and, second, they have several avenues at their disposal to collect that debt.

The first avenue they can use to collect a debt is a tax lien. A lien is the government's claim on the taxpayer's property.

The law generally defines a lien as a charge of encumbrance that one person has on the property of another as security for a debt, in this case a federal **or** state tax debt.

Liens, as it states in the IRS guidebook, the *Internal Revenue Manual* (§5.17.2.2, revised on 3/19/18), can be categorized into three types: Common Law, Consensual and Statutory.

General liens are also called "silent liens."

Why silent?

As the name implies, no one is notified of the issuance of the lien when it is placed on the county records. The IRS does not notify the tax debtor when the lien is placed, nor does it notify any credit reporting agencies, for that matter. However, rest assured, the credit bureaus do find out and the debtor's credit score can be impacted, typically some 30 to 35 points or more.

According to an article on CreditKarma.com, the exact impact depends on several factors. Those factors are:

- How old the lien is

- Which scoring model is used and how heavily each weighs on that lien

  - Vantage Score 3.0®

  - FICO®

- Whether the lien is paid or still open

However, it should be noted that, in July 2017, the credit bureaus (Experian, Transunion, and Equifax) removed the judgement date as well as about half of all tax lien data reports. This is based on a report by the National Consumer Protection Agency that recommended making credit reports more consumer-friendly and accurate, with the removal of old, paid-off liens, for example. As such, as of April 16, 2018, the three credit bureaus announced that tax lien data will not be reported. As many as 11% of Americans with tax liens saw a rise in their credit score by as much as 30 points, practically overnight.

Be aware that just because the three credit bureaus do not report a tax lien, it does not mean the lien does not exist. It hasn't magically disappeared as if it passed through the Bermuda Triangle; it is on the county records and, if not paid, is still very much active... which means collection activity by the IRS will continue.
All hands on deck!

When the tax debt is $10,000 or more, the government places this lien against all property you currently own or will own. Believe it or not, this is actually an improvement in your favor. Prior to the enactment of the Fresh Start Initiative, the threshold for triggering a lien was only $5,000 – half of what it is now. At least we're moving in the right direction, folks!

I want to address a common misconception regarding liens. This is that the IRS will take your property once a lien is in place. That is where confusion arises between a lien and levy.

You might be asking what authority gave the Internal Revenue Service the right to issue these silent liens? Congress, that's who, as codified in §6321. However, the silent lien has a low priority. That honor goes to the NFTL, the Notice of Federal Tax Lien, which we will discuss later.

The lien remains in effect up to the earlier of the date the debt is paid in full or the Collections Statute of Limitations (CSOL) expires. This is also known as the Collection Statute Expiration Date, or CSED.

The CSED is generally 10 years from the date the return is filed, which is when the tax is self-assessed (as mentioned earlier). Per statute (the law), the IRS cannot collect on a tax debt that is 10 or more years old. It is then "written off" and the lien should be removed. Prior to that, any tax return overpayment, whether you ask for a refund or request that it be applied to the next year's tax, is used as an offset against a past tax debt.

As quoted in the IRS' *Internal Revenue Manual* in §5.1.19, "Each tax assessment has a Collection Statute Expiration Date (CSED). Internal Revenue Code section 6502 provides that the length of the period for collection after assessment of a tax liability is 10 years. The collection statute expiration ends the government's right to pursue collection of a liability."

I must make you aware that any statute is not absolute. This is a perfect case in point. In certain circumstances, the collection statute expiration date can be extended beyond the 10 years for a variety of reasons.

Certain actions can "stop the clock" on collection activity, which extends the time that the IRS is allowed to collect. This stopping of the clock is called tolling. Everything comes to standstill – the IRS has its anchor moored and it's not coming after you...for now.

Actions that can Trigger Tolling, or What Stops the Clock

- Leaving the Country

  - If you are thinking about leaving the country for a few years to allow the clock to run out... think again. The CSED stops running when you hit international waters, and it stays stopped for the entire time you are outside our borders. You may ask how will the IRS even know that I'm gone? Trust me, they know. They know because they share information with both Customs and Homeland Security.

- Bankruptcy Filing

  - The CSED is tolled while your case is in progress, whether you are filing for a chapter 7 or chapter 13. So, if the debt isn't discharged as a result of the bankruptcy (and not all tax debt is dischargeable... but that's for another book), the IRS will be waiting, and it will be waiting at the same spot on the clock.

- Request was Made for "Separation of Joint and Several Liability" (§6015, et al)

  - This is done via an innocent spouse filing.

  - This means that one spouse claims that the other spouse should be held solely responsible for the tax.

- Offer In Compromise

  - If you think the IRS collection department or the IRS Revenue Officer is encouraging you to file an offer in compromise because you are a good candidate for one, you are probably mistaken. Filing an offer allows the IRS to see all of your financial history and stops the clock from running. In the IRS Revenue Officer's mind, your income may be going up while you wait for the offer to be rejected (55% to 60% are rejected) and he or she will be waiting at the end with the same amount of time to collect as when you filed the offer.

- Collection Due Process Hearing Request

  - The IRS must issue a "final" notice of intent to levy before it can hit your bank account and paycheck. When it does, an opportunity arises for you to appeal collection and propose alternatives, such as a payment plan or an OIC. The problem with a CDP hearing request is that the CSED is tolled after it is filed, and the tolling continues until the hearing is over, which may be a long time if you use the right to appeal or go to tax court.

- Installment Agreement Request

  - The clock stops while the IRS is considering your Installment Agreement Request.

- Fraud

  - You can't defend an IRS collection suit by arguing that the CSED has run out if it was your own fraud that prevented collection in the first place.

- Someone Else has Your Stuff

- The CSED is tolled when your things are in the control or custody of a court (which is, arguably, someone else), or even by the IRS in some circumstances (i.e., wrongful seizure).

- You can also agree to extend the statute, though this is a very rare occurrence.

What happens if there is plenty of time to go on the CSED and you have not paid, requested payment plans, or have just plain ignored any of the letters from the Internal Revenue Service? The IRS issues a series of letters.

You may want to refer to my first book (in print, Kindle, and audio book), *Now What? I Received a Tax Notice from the IRS. Help*! (https://www.amazon.com/What-Notice-IRS-Help-Life-preserving/dp/0692997156). There, you will find a complete list of IRS notices as well as explanations of what each means to you.

The notice I am specifically referring to is IRS Notice CP 504, Notice of Intent to Levy. This is the notice that you have a **balance due** on your tax account. The IRS will have previously sent you notices about a balance due. This urgent notice again alerts you that there is an outstanding balance, and the IRS **intends** to levy or take your state tax refunds.

If you ignore this, the "fun" begins.

Besides taking your refund from a future return (even without sending you various notices other than a past tax due notice), there are many other ways that the IRS can get the money that is owed to them. At some point, they can levy your bank accounts, garnish your wages, social security benefits, and pensions payments, or, if applicable, take state tax refunds.

Unbeknownst to many, the IRS and various state departments of revenue have agreements with each other. These agreements are a part of the Federal Offset Program which we will go over in detail later.

Though the CP504 is serious notice and should be addressed immediately, this notice does not have the authority to actually levy your assets. That honor belongs to the IRS CP90/CP297 notices. However, it is serious enough for the IRS to notify you that your assets or wages can be put into play if the back taxes are ignored. However, it is "just" a notice that the IRS intends to levy, not that they will, YET!

Think of it this way: getting a CP 504 notice means that the winds are picking up and the clouds are rolling in ... there's a storm ahead.
An LT1058 or LT11 notice means the storm is upon you ... take evasive action NOW or lose it all!

The Internal Revenue Code (§6330) requires that the IRS send a **"Final Notice – Notice of Intent To Levy And Notice Of Your Right To A Hearing" (IRS CP90/CP297.)** before they take action. The IRS cannot actually issue a levy or seize your property until they advise you that you have a right to an appeal via a Collection Due Process Hearing (CDP). However, the CP504 does not say that. However, it does state that you have 30 days to make arrangements to pay the tax, penalties and interest. The LT1058 or LT11 notice has this specific language (it is in the actual header of the notice).

This will give you time to consult with your experienced tax professional to gather the necessary information needed to determine your course of action; to pay the tax in full, or pay a lesser amount negotiated in a partial pay installment arrangement or an offer in compromise.

A CDP allows you to present the facts demonstrating that you cannot pay the tax. You are taking advantage of the collections due process when you voluntarily apply for any of the other collection alternatives at your disposal: apply to be placed in currently not collectible or CNC status, request a full pay installment plan, a partial pay installment agreement (PPIA), or an Offer in Compromise (OIC).

If you have to file all the same forms and provide the same documentation whether you request a CDP or not, why go through the hassle and expense (unless you are representing yourself, which is not highly recommended)? It preserves your judicial rights to go to tax court. Not that you would go before a U.S. Tax Court Judge, as many do not, but if you want to, you cannot if you miss the deadline of the CDP. If you miss the deadline, there is an alternative; a request for an equivalent hearing. However, if you do this, you cannot then go to tax court.

As I stated before, most tax court petitions do not make it to court, as they are remanded (sent back) to the appeals division.

Requesting a CDP stops all "enforced" collections. No more letters, no more threats (except maybe from the Appeals officer who will be hearing your case). They will request the data by a certain date and set up a hearing date, which can be over the phone (if assigned to a campus) or in person (highly recommended).

The downside to all of this is that the clock stops ticking while the hearing is in play. Therefore, you and your representative must be cognizant of the dates for the various statutes of limitations, especially the CSED.

Does this let you off the hook? Not so fast, Kimosabe.

You will not get collection notices and your assets will not be levied, nor will your wages be garnished. However, it is only temporary if you cannot come to an agreement with Appeals officer. You have a matter of weeks, not months, to figure out what you want to do.

So, what is the real difference between the LT1058 and LT11 notices? The LT11 is a final notice of intent to seize your property, not just take your money. Semantics? Maybe, but to the IRS is it is a big difference. However, like the LT1058, you have 30 days to request a CDP hearing.

CHAPTER 7

Levy – to Impose a Tax, the Amount Owed to the IRS

After all the notices are sent (and received?), the threats that the Internal Revenue Service will come to take your property start to become real. The IRS is commandeering your ship and pirating your stuff.

The most common method by which the IRS does this is called a levy or seizure. Simply stated, a levy is where the IRS takes your property in order to pay off a tax debt you owe.

The question is, what can they levy?

Two of the most common types of levies are a bank levy and a wage garnishment. The IRS will issue a levy notice to all the banks that they find under your name and social security number (and believe me, they know) and request that X number of dollars be handed over to them.

If you don't have enough money to cover your outstanding tax debt, the amount the IRS levies is whatever is in the account on the day of the levy.

As stated in IRS publication 594, after the levy is issued, the bank will hold the available funds and give you 21 days to resolve any disputes about who owns the account before sending the money to the IRS. After 21 days, the bank will send the money to the IRS, along with any interest earned on that amount, unless you have resolved the issue in some other way.

Generally, notices regarding levies are mailed by regular mail... so don't ignore your mailbox!

The IRS generally uses Form 668–A(C)DO to levy property that a third party is holding, such as a bank or even business receivables.

As I said before, the money to be turned over is the amount requested on the day the levy notice is issued. If you win the lottery the next day, or the day after they take the money, they cannot touch that cash – unless the Internal Revenue Service issues another levy.

However, before they execute the levy, the IRS has to send you a bill entitled **"Final Notice – Notice of Intent To Levy And Notice Of Your Right To A Hearing"** via Form LT1058. Anyone who receives this IRS bill should immediately send out an SOS to a tax professional such as an Enrolled Agent or CPA, one that is experienced in these issues, as you only have a short window (30 days) to save your ship. By doing so, you may be able to make arrangements to pay the liability or enter into one of the collection alternatives, instead of having the IRS proceed with the levy.

It's also important that those who receive a levy for their employees, vendors, customers, or other third parties comply with it. Failure to do so may subject the party receiving the levy to personal liability for the levy.

When the IRS is in the Wrong - You're Guilty Until Proven Innocent

Normally you would only have the 30 days to take action before the IRS levies your property after you receive Form LT1058. However, the IRS gives individuals and businesses additional time to file an administrative claim or to bring a civil action for wrongful levy or seizure.

In fact, The Tax Cuts and Jobs Act of 2017 enacted in December of that year, extended the time limit for filing an administrative claim as well as for bringing a suit for wrongful levy from nine months to two years.

If an administrative claim for return of the property is made within the two-year period, the two-year period for bringing a suit is extended for 12 months from the date of filing of the claim or for six months from the disallowance of the claim, whichever is shorter. The change in law applies to levies made after December 22, 2017, and, on or before that date, if the previous nine-month period hadn't yet expired.

The timeframes apply when the IRS has already sold the property it levied. As under prior law, there is no time limit for an administrative claim if the IRS still has the property it levied. Also, taxpayers may not file a wrongful levy claim or bring a wrongful levy suit, as the law only applies to those other than the taxpayer. Usually, wrongful levy claims involve situations where an individual or business believes that either the property belongs to them, or they have a superior claim to the property that the IRS is not recognizing.

To file an administrative wrongful levy claim, send a letter to the IRS Advisory Group for the area where the levy was made. For a list of Advisory Group offices, see Publication 4235, *Collection Advisory Group Numbers and Addresses*, available on IRS.gov.

If, following a claim, the IRS determines it has wrongfully levied property, it will return one of the following:

- the property,
- an amount of money equal to the amount of money levied, or
- an amount of money equal to the money received from the sale of the property.

Anyone whose wrongful levy claim is denied by the IRS has the right to appeal through the agency's Collection Appeals Program.

Hitting You Where it Hurts: Your Paycheck

The next most common levy method is wage garnishment. This is where the IRS instructs your employer to withhold money from your check each period and hand it over to the IRS.

As you can imagine, a wage garnishment causes the most angst to the taxpayer. The employee walks into their place of employment and gets called into their HR department – or, worse, their boss's office – and is told that the money will be withheld from his or her paycheck. I am sure that this is money you really can't afford to lose. If you employer does receive a notice, they have no choice but to take care of it immediately.

The IRS uses Form 668–W(ICS) or 668-W(C)DO to levy an individual's wages, salary (including fees, bonuses, commissions, and similar items), or other income. Form 668-W(ICS) and/or 668-W(C)(DO) also provides notice of a levy on a taxpayer's benefit or retirement income.

Your employer will receive a Form 668-W(ICS) or 668-W(C)DO, Notice of Levy on Wages, Salary and Other Income (or other levy form) before they are required to withhold and send any funds from your wages to the IRS.

The Internal Revenue Code allows for continuous levies with respect to wages, salaries and certain other types of property. This means that a levy on wages and salaries continuously attaches until it is released. Examples of property continuously attached include:

- Salary and wages

- Deferred compensation payments, such as retirement or pension income

In the case of a levy on wages, your employer will pay you any amount exempt from the levy. The IRS calculates the exempt amount based on the standard deduction and the number of personal exemptions the employee is allowed.

IRS Publication 1494, which is mailed with Form 668-W(ICS) or 668-W(C)DO, explains to the employer how to compute the amount exempt from levy. A levy includes a Statement of Exemptions and Filing Status. The employer gives this statement to the employee to complete and return within three days. If the employer does not receive the statement in three days, the exempt amount is figured as if the person is married filing separately with one exemption. The IRS will notify the employer when the taxpayer is not entitled to exemptions to the levy.

The amount withheld from your paycheck can be further reduced by court ordered payments like child support and alimony Just be aware, you are allowed to keep some of your pay, but it may not be enough to live on. Refer to Publication 1494 that the IRS will send you, via https://www.irs.gov/pub/irs-pdf/p1494.pdf, or in the withholding amounts exhibit in this book.

If a wage levy continues from one calendar year to the next, the employee may submit a new Statement of Exemptions and Filing Status and ask their employer to re-compute the exempt amount. I have included an exhibit of this here as well as in the appendix.

1. Tables for Figuring Amount Exempt from Levy on Wages, Salary, and Other Income (Forms 668-W(ACS), 668-W(c)(DO) and 668-W(ICS))
The tables below show the amount of an individual's income (take home pay) that is exempt from a notice of levy used to collect delinquent tax in 2018 — **2018**

Filing Status: Single

Pa	0	1	2	3	4	5	More Than 5
Daily	46.15	62.11	78.07	94.03	109.99	125.95	46.15 plus 15.96 for each dependent
Weekly	230.77	310.58	390.39	470.20	550.01	629.82	230.77 plus 79.81 for each dependent
Biweekly	461.54	621.16	780.78	940.40	1100.02	1259.64	461.54 plus 159.62 for each dependent
Semimonthly	500.00	672.92	845.84	1018.76	1191.68	1364.60	500.00 plus 172.92 for each dependent
Monthly	1000.00	1345.83	1691.66	2037.49	2383.32	2729.15	1000.00 plus 345.83 for each dependent

Filing Status: Married Filing Joint Return (and Qualifying Widow(er)s)

Pa	0	1	2	3	4	5	More Than 5
Daily	92.31	108.27	124.33	140.19	156.15	172.11	93.21 plus 15.96 for each dependent
Weekly	461.54	541.35	621.16	700.97	780.78	860.59	461.54 plus 79.81 for each dependent
Biweekly	923.08	1082.70	1242.32	1401.94	1561.56	1721.18	923.08 plus 159.62 for each dependent
Semimonthly	1000.00	1172.92	1345.84	1518.76	1691.68	1864.60	1000.00 plus 172.92 for each dependent
Monthly	2000.00	2345.83	2691.66	3037.49	3383.32	3729.15	2000.00 plus 345.83 for each dependent

Filing Status: Head of Household

Pa	0	1	2	3	4	5	More Than 5
Daily	69.23	85.19	101.15	117.11	133.07	149.03	69.23 plus 15.96 for each dependent
Weekly	346.15	425.96	505.87	585.68	665.49	745.30	346.15 plus 79.81 for each dependent
Biweekly	692.31	851.93	1011.55	1171.17	1330.79	1490.41	692.31 plus 159.62 for each dependent
Semimonthly	750.00	922.92	1095.84	1268.76	1441.88	1614.60	750.00 plus 172.92 for each dependent
Monthly	1500.00	1845.83	2191.66	2537.49	2883.32	3229.15	1500.00 + 345.83 for each dependent

Filing Status: Married Filing Separate Return

Pa	0	1	2	3	4	5	More Than 5
Daily	46.15	62.11	78.07	94.03	109.99	125.95	46.15 plus 15.96 for each dependent
Weekly	230.77	310.58	390.39	470.20	550.01	629.82	230.77 plus 79.81 for each dependent
Biweekly	461.54	621.16	780.78	940.40	1100.02	1259.64	461.54 plus 159.62 for each dependent
Semimonthly	500.00	672.92	845.84	1018.76	1191.68	1364.80	500.00 plus 172.92 for each dependent
Monthly	1000.00	1345.83	1691.66	2037.49	2383.32	2729.15	1000.00 + 345.83 for each dependent

Your Business and Tax Debt

You may be wondering if the same IRS rules apply to businesses as they do to individuals. Will the IRS levy your business?

Let's talk first about LLCs, or Limited Liability Companies. LLCs have become very popular over the past decade (or more), as they give taxpayers several filing options and benefits. This is because they are considered "disregarded entities."

In other words, the way in which an LLC is taxed depends entirely upon how you set it up (structure it) and whether the members (another name for the owners or, in corporate terms, the shareholders) make an election to have it treated in a particular way for tax purposes.

For example, a single member LLC (no other owners or partners, though it can have multiple officers or managers) can be treated as either a corporation or a sole proprietorship. If the single member does not make a special election, the LLC is, by default, treated as a sole proprietorship. A multi-member LLC can be treated as either a partnership or a corporation. If no election is made, by default, the multi-member LLC is considered a partnership. You should consult your experienced tax advisor on the best way to tax yourself, as every circumstance is different. You should talk with an attorney experienced in liability protection to determine whether should you "organize" as an LLC or "incorporate" your entity. He or she will advise you based on the state (or states) in which you are conducting business as well as on what is best for your business model.

Let's say that you did organize as an LLC and you did not elect to be taxed as a corporation on the advice of your advisors. If the LLC structure is "disregarded," why bother to set it up in the first place? Understand that the term "disregarded" applies only to the way the entity is treated for federal income tax purposes.

Since LLCs became a creature of state law and have fallen into favor with attorneys and tax advisors, Congress has not seen fit to amend the tax laws to expressly provide the way that they are taxed. (By contrast, the tax code spends hundreds of pages addressing how corporations, partnerships, trusts and sole proprietorships are to be taxed).

The question of how LLCs are taxed was therefore made a matter of regulation. LLCs are given the option to simply elect how they are to be treated for tax purposes, and the IRS must live with that election.

So, what happens to an LLC if a member owes federal income taxes? If the LLC is disregarded for tax purposes, can the IRS reach through the LLC veil and seize the assets of the company to pay the debts of the member? Is it not the reason to set up a separate legal entity (LLC or corporation) to protect your personal assets from corporate issues or to protect the entity's assets from personal issues? This has become a concern, particularly as the IRS gets more aggressive with the collection of debts.

Let's compare the LLC to a corporation similar to an LLC, a corporation is a separate legal entity under state law. The corporation's shareholders (and especially the officers or employees) do not own the corporation's assets, they own only their stock in the corporation. Although they can receive dividends or distributions (if they elected to be taxed as an S-corporation; check with your tax advisor for details), no shareholder can walk into an office of the business, present his or her stock certificates to the administrative assistant, and walk out with his or her share of the office furniture or heaven forbid their cash.

It is the same in the other direction. If a shareholder of, say, Microsoft (Gates or otherwise) owes money to the IRS, the IRS cannot seize any of the corporation's income or assets to satisfy that debt. The IRS *can* seize the shareholder's stock and sell it, but generally (unless it is a controlling shareholder like Gates), it has no effect on the corporation. Also, if Microsoft declares a dividend and the IRS still owns the stock it took from the debtor shareholder, the IRS will get the dividend. That is the extent to which the IRS can mess with the business.

Is the answer the same for an LLC? The IRS sometimes argues that if it's dealing with a single member LLC, and the single member owes taxes, the IRS can seize the assets of the LLC because it's a disregarded entity and there's just one owner. That is, the IRS just looks past (or "disregards") the LLC status.

However, the IRS is dead wrong.

Being a disregarded entity is how the entity is taxed, it does not change who owns the assets. Therefore, if the LLC owns the assets, the IRS has no claim to those assets to settle a member's tax debt. When it comes to the ownership issue, the IRS must look to state law to determine whether a person has an ownership interest in any particular asset. There is a long-standing case that was ruled on in the US Supreme Court in 1960 that holds this as true (Aquilino v. United States, 363 U.S. 509). If state law does not allow for an ownership interest in an asset in favor of the person who owes the tax, the IRS cannot seize that asset.

Thus, there is the question of state law. Does it create an ownership interest in the assets of an LLC in favor of a member? This question has to be answered on a state-by-state basis, but, generally speaking, the answer is no. The reason I say no is that it is the very idea behind an LLC. The structure is, by definition, a separate legal entity capable of owning its own assets, just like a corporation. The 90

LLC's assets are not (and should not be) commingled with those if its members. If that were not true, there'd be no point to having a Limited Liability Company.

Another problem with single-member LLCs is with collection cases. Is the LLC just the "alter ego" of the member? What this means is that if the LLC is merely treated as an extension of a single person, to the extent that the entity and individual's activities are practically indistinguishable one from another, then the entity and individual should be treated as a single individual with no limited liability. In other words, the entity is "dominated" or used as an instrument for a sole individual's purposes.

In this author's opinion, to avoid being considered an alter ego, the LLC's assets are not (and should) not) be commingled with those of its members. If that were not true, there'd be no point in having a Limited Liability Company.

However, the question of whether the LLC protection can be pierced is also largely an issue controlled by state law. There has been substantial law created in this area over the years, as the IRS has been highly successful in piercing trusts and corporations for tax collection purposes under certain circumstances.

Thus, it is not a common occurrence, but the IRS will try to do what they have to do collect a debt. One suggestion that I give to all my clients, is this: In order to make your entity as credit adverse as possible, do not comingle funds (as mentioned earlier) do not pay personal expenses out of the entity, and try not to link business bank accounts with your personal accounts. Even though, banks

should not allow this (per their own rules), I have seen it happen…
much to my chagrin.

CHAPTER 8

What Else Can They Do When Your Ship is Taking on Water?

If this happens, it is time to consult with a more experienced person to steer your sinking ship!

Other than a levy, a seizure, or a wage garnishment, how else can the IRS get paid (once, of course, they determine that the debtor is not paying what they owe or making other arrangements)?

The IRS can also issue garnishment orders against your social security income. I have one client that is having 100% of their social security payments garnished (they owed over seven figures, that is, over $1 million) before other arrangements were made. Another client was just notified that "only" 15% of their benefits will be levied. We beat that, however, as we had an installment agreement approved on the $30,000 debt.

Another means of collection by the IRS that you may not be aware of is tapping your accounts receivable if you own a business. In other words, they can go after the money that your customers or clients owe you. Believe it or not, the Internal Revenue Service can sail right past you, contacting these businesses and individuals directly and requiring them to pay what you owe to the IRS instead of to your business. As you can imagine, this can be rather humiliating.

At this point in our journey together you may be starting to ask how far the IRS can go. For example, can the IRS seize your home or other real estate you own? The simple answer is yes, they can. The seizure of a taxpayer's home or business is authorized by the Internal Revenue Code.

With merely a stroke of a pen, the IRS District Director is empowered to take a taxpayer's home or business. The Internal Revenue Service Restructuring and Reform Act of 1998 (1998 Tax Act) extended the District Director's privilege to seize homes and businesses to all U.S. District Court Judges and Magistrates, and only provides lifeboats for taxpayers owing $5,000 or less. Everyone else is going down with the ship on this one.

If you owe the IRS more than the safe harbor amount of $5,000 and do not pay in a timely manner, the IRS can take your home and business in a public sale.

The IRS must follow specific procedures in seizing a taxpayer's home or business, as laid out in the following sections of the IRS's *Internal Revenue Manual*: Part 5., Collecting Process; Chapter 10., Seizure and Sale; and Section 3., Conducting the Seizure.

First, the IRS must ask your permission to enter your premises. If you wish to allow the IRS to enter and seize your home or business, you simply sign your name to a short form and walk away.

If you refuse to give permission, however, the IRS will apply for a seizure order with a U.S. District Court Judge or Magistrate. Once the judge has read and approved the IRS's request for a seizure order, IRS agents revisit your property, and may even be carrying weapons.

You will be allowed to collect your personal effects, including tools and equipment needed for your employment or your job. All the IRS really wants is the real estate. The IRS will then padlock the premises, post notices to the public, and arrange to sell the home or business assets to the highest bidder.

If you take a look at the IRS auction site at https://www.treasury.gov/auctions/irs/, you will see that there is very little that the IRS is prohibited from seizing. Exempt assets are usually confined to small items of minimal value.

Let me provide a real-life example of just how powerful the IRS is when it comes to seizing money and property. A friend of mine worked for the IRS as a Revenue Officer (RO). Remember, an RO has a job to do: collect tax on behalf of the IRS and U.S. government. In this case, the taxpayer owed quite a substantial amount of money (in the seven-figure range) and refused to cooperate with the IRS. In his investigation, the RO determined that the taxpayer owned planes (that's right, planes, as in more than one). So, this RO went to the airfield, bringing with him all the proper approvals needed. He slapped a notice on the planes which stated that they now belong to the U.S. government. The taxpayer chose to pay the tax rather than lose his planes. Yes, I oversimplified the story, but I hope you get the gist of the situation, and yes, this case had to do with a lot of money, and maybe you and I cannot just write a check, **but** it doesn't diminish the fact that the IRS has the right to do this… to all taxpayers.

Maybe the IRS won't take your house, your boat, or your plane, but they will levy, garnish, and seize.

That being said, IRS seizures of homes, personal assets (like a plane or boat), and businesses are often unnecessary, and sometimes even illegal. Seizures can be caused by ill feelings and poor communication between the taxpayer and the IRS collector.

Most people who owe taxes can negotiate a satisfactory solution with IRS collectors. Again, there are collection alternatives (mentioned earlier) that were made available under the Fresh Start Program. I will address these in more detail in the next section.

There are, however, some items that cannot be commandeered (seized) by the long arm of the Internal Revenue Service. Previously, I mentioned that the IRS must allow you to keep a minimal amount on a wage garnishment. I also mentioned that certain court-ordered payments are exempt, such as alimony or spousal support and child support. However, the full list of items that are exempt as provided in Internal Revenue Code §6334 is shown on the following list:

1. Wearing apparel (clothes) and school books - necessary for the taxpayer or for members of his family;

2. Fuel, provisions, furniture, and personal effects in the taxpayer's household and arms for personal use, livestock, and poultry of the taxpayer, if it does not exceed $6,250 in value;

3. Books and tools necessary for a trade, business, or profession, if it does not exceed in the aggregate $3,125 in value.

4. Unemployment benefits of any amount that are payable to an individual with respect to his unemployment (including any portion with respect to dependents) paid by any state, District of Columbia, or Puerto Rico.

5. Undelivered mail addressed to any person, which has not been delivered to the addressee.

6. Certain annuity and pension payments under the Railroad Unemployment Insurance Act, special pension payments received by a person whose name has been entered on the Army, Navy, Air Force, and Coast Guard Medal of Honor Roll, and annuities based on retirement or retainer pay under chapter 73 of title 10 of the United States Code (retired serviceman's family protection plan or survivor benefits).

7. Workmen's compensation payable to an individual as workmen's compensation (including any portion thereof payable with respect to dependents) under a workers' compensation law of the United States, any State, the District of Columbia, or the Commonwealth of Puerto Rico.

8. Judgments for support of minor children if the taxpayer is required by judgment of a court of competent jurisdiction, entered prior to the date of levy, to contribute to the support of his minor children, so much of his salary, wages, or other income as is necessary to comply with such judgment.

9. Minimum exemptions for wages, salary, and other income payable to or received by an individual as wages or salary for personal services, or as income derived from other sources, during any period, to the extent that the total of such amounts payable to or received by him or her during such period does not exceed the applicable exempt amount.

10. Certain service-connected disability payments payable to an individual.

11. Certain public assistance payments payable to an individual as a recipient of public assistance under:

(A) Title IV or title XVI (relating to supplemental security income for the aged, blind, and disabled) of the Social Security Act, or

(B) State or local government public assistance or public welfare programs for which eligibility is determined by a needs or income test

12. Assistance under the Job Training Partnership Act in the amount payable to a participant under the Job Training Partnership Act.

CHAPTER 9

Levy Release: When the IRS Stops Taking Your Bounty

Once the IRS starts to levy your assets, the agency will continue to take assets until the tax debt is paid in full.

How do you get a levy released if you cannot pay your tax debt in full? As I mentioned throughout this book, there are several collection alternatives.

You have heard the commercials – "We can save you up to 85% of the tax you owe if you qualify." That is true, though it can be much more, or much less.

Just be careful of anyone who says that they will save you pennies on the dollar. Again, that statement can be true, it just depends on *how many* pennies.

Also, the disclaimer is "*if you qualify.*" These are mainly directed toward Offers in Compromise (OIC) where you pay an amount less than what you actually owe. Many do not qualify, as 55% to 60%

of submitted offers do not get accepted. Although the success rate (40% to 45%) is terrific for major league baseball players, it is not really a high success rate in real life. Consider this, if you consistently succeed 45% of the time in your job, school or other sports, then you would most likely be considered a failure. Also, that does not count all the taxpayers going to a taxpayer representative thinking that they can get an Offer, but do not qualify. It is easier to get an offer accepted than it was a few years ago (when success rates were in the 30% range), but it is still a tough road when you want to pay less than what you owe.

Once the offer is accepted, your debt is removed from your account and cannot come back to haunt you… as long as you pay your taxes (including any required estimated tax payments) and file your returns on time for five consecutive years. If not, your offer is cancelled and your debt is placed back on the books.

If you do not qualify for an OIC, you can also enter into what we call a structured payment plan. Another name for this is an Installment Agreement.

If the taxpayer's income, minus certain expenses (called "net disposable income") can pay the taxes owed within 72 months or before the collection statute expires (or over 72 months), whichever is less, then they can enter into a full-pay installment arrangement. If not, then they can enter into a partial-pay installment.

What are considered "certain expenses?" They are related to what the IRS considers to be national and local standards, which change every March, and spell out exactly what the IRS says you can spend on housing, food, utilities, car costs and ownership, etc. These standards may not have anything to do with reality, but they are what they are. Any amounts that are over these standards may qualify, but only under certain, limited circumstances.

The final collection alternative is called Currently Non-Collectible, or CNC. This is where your net disposable income is close to or at zero, you cannot afford an offer, and you do not have any borrowing power. The IRS puts your account on "stasis," which means no collections or letters, except the annual form that tells you how much you owe. The IRS will perform periodic checks to see if your income goes up from one year to the next. If so, they will require you to enter into one of the other alternatives as discussed previously.

When you enter into an offer in compromise, any refund expected in the year in which you apply for the OIC and in the year of acceptance (these can take up to 24 months to be accepted, though they generally only take six months or so), will be applied to the debt, not the offer. In the case of the installment agreements or CNC, any overpayments will be applied to your debt until the debt is paid. This is where great tax planning is needed. The IRS will not refund any money while you owe them an outstanding balance. This is part of the Federal Offset Program.

While your choice of collection alternatives is being considered, interest and penalties continue to accrue. However (and most importantly) the enforced collections (liens, levies, etc.) will stop, for the time being.

Another viable option (not one that the IRS openly discusses) is filing for bankruptcy. You must realize, though, that not all back taxes are dischargeable. I am not an attorney and you will need competent representation if you go this route and I am not giving legal advice, but the Bankruptcy Code requires that specific time periods be met in order to discharge your taxes. These are commonly called the 3-year, 2-year, and 240-day rules (the "3-2-240 rules"). Under these rules, you can discharge income taxes that came due three years before you filed for bankruptcy. If you get an extension of time to file, the three-year period runs from the date that the taxes are due under the extension, if it has been at least two years since you filed the tax forms *and* 240 days since the taxes were assessed. As always, there are some exceptions. Rules also do not apply to all types of taxes, for example, they do not apply to property or payroll taxes.

There are other considerations (such as general unsecured debt, priority tax debt or secured tax debt), but all of that goes beyond the scope of this book.

One other issue that can be a concern is what I call the "one-and-done" rule. The IRS will fight the bankruptcy if your return is even *one day* late or if they filed a Substitute for Return for you. What is a Substitute for Return? The IRS has the information to create a return for you and can assess a tax based on its records (i.e., W2s, 1099s, etc.). When they do this, they do not give you itemized deductions, dependents, credits or allow for you file jointly, however. They believe that if you file late or that if they have to come after you, the associated taxes should not be discharged. So far, the IRS has taken all these taxpayers to circuit court and has won each and every time.

CHAPTER 10

What Happens to the Seized Property? Can I Get My Stuff Back?!

As indicated in Section 3, the IRS will sell your interest in the property it seizes.

Remember, if you own property jointly with a non-liable person, they will become part owners of that property (i.e., real estate, business ownership), making it harder to sell it outright. The IRS will try to sell their newfound interest.

However, prior to doing any such thing, the IRS must provide the debtor with a copy of how they calculated the minimum bid. This gives you a chance to challenge their numbers if you feel they are too low.

The IRS will also publish a notice of the pending sale, mainly in local newspapers, and even post flyers in public places. They generally wait 10 days before selling the seized asset.

Money from the sale is first applied to the cost of the seizing and selling said property. The rest of the proceeds will be applied against the debt. Any amount remaining can be refunded to the debtor. The Internal Revenue Service has very specific rules (of course, they do) on how to do that.

If the debtor wishes to get their property back once it is seized, they must contact the IRS to resolve the debt. The IRS will not entertain any release until either the debt is paid or one of the collection alternatives is offered (no pun intended). If this occurs, you can request that the property be released and returned to you.

Any adverse decision in this process can be appealed. Remember, the Taxpayer Bill of Rights? The first paragraph in that section, says it all:

Taxpayers are entitled to a fair and impartial administrative appeal of most IRS decisions, including many penalties, and have the right to receive a written response regarding the Office of Appeals' decision. Taxpayers generally have the right to take their cases to court.

The IRS is required to release any seized property if it determines that:

1. You paid the amount you owe;

2. The collection statute ended **before** the notice of seizure was issued;

3. Releasing the seizure would help pay your taxes (for example, you can get a better price in a private sale than in an IRS auction);

4. You entered into a structured payment plan;

5. The seizure creates an economic hardship;

6. The value of the property is more than the amount owed and the release will not hinder the collection of the tax owed.

Although the above is about released/returned property, it does not apply to previously garnished wages, social security, pension benefits, or previously-taken money from a bank account due to a levy being issued. Once the money is taken and applied, it is gone… if it was done in accordance with the law and regulations. If it was done in error (dare we say illegally), you can make a claim for a refund or sue in United States Tax Court or District Court.

CHAPTER 11

What is the Treasury Offset Program?
Looting What's Onboard to Pay Your Debt

It's a great disappearing act... you had a refund coming, and POOF! now you don't. Instead, you get a notice that says it was applied to your outstanding balance. This is a prime example of the Treasury Offset Program or "TOP."

The Treasury Offset Program (TOP) is a program run by the U.S. Department of Treasury through the Bureau of Fiscal Services Debt Management System. Its primary purpose is to collect debts owed to various Federal agencies and to the states (not to be confused with the IRS applying an overpayment in one year against a prior year's tax debt).

So how does TOP work?

It is authorized pursuant to 31 USC§371(6)(c), which gives the Bureau of Fiscal Services the responsibility for issuing federal payments, including tax refunds.

As I indicated, the IRS gets first crack at any tax overpayment, applying it to back tax debts before issuing any current refund or allowing an overpayment to be applied to the next year's tax.

Also, if you owe back taxes and file an amended return, any subsequent overpayment will be used to offset back taxes. When I discussed offers in compromise, I mentioned that, in the year of making the offer and in the year of acceptance (if the process crosses more than one year) any refund will be kept and applied to the debt and it does not reduce to the offer.

What happens if you are in default to another federal or state agency, such as being behind on a student loan or on your child support? The Bureau of Fiscal Services may use some or all of your current year's federal income tax overpayment (or even a prior year as indicated on an amended return) to pay down that obligation.

How do they do this? Generally, the Federal agency, for example, the U.S. Department of Education, submits delinquent debts for collection to be included in TOP. The debt is then certified, qualifying it for collection by an offset. The affected agency prepares and certifies payment vouchers which contain information pertaining to the debtor, such as their name and identification number, etc.

As this is a centralized system, TOP is handled by one agency. Before issuing a refund the system "checks" the records to see if a creditor agency has submitted a voucher that matches the name and taxpayer identification number, or TIN. (A TIN is a social security number for an individual or a federal employee identification number, or FEIN, for a business).

If the TIN and the name on the voucher matches the TIN and the name of the debtor, the disbursing official offsets (applies) the payment, in whole or in part, to satisfy the obligation (tax debt).

Now is a good time to state that not all delinquent debts can be part of the offset program. There are many code sections governing these debts, specifying which ones can be offset and which ones cannot. This part of the book will address which debts can be offset as a part of the program. I have already mentioned two: student loans and child support.

In any case, once the Bureau of Fiscal Services determines that an offset is warranted, the bureau withholds the money to be applied to the obligation and transmits it to the affected agency or agencies. The Bureau of Fiscal Services keeps information about the debtor and the delinquent debt in the TOP Delinquent Debtor Database. They continue to monitor these records and continue to offset refunds until the creditor agency suspends or terminates collection activity.

A creditor agency will suspend collection if the debt is subject to a bankruptcy petition or if other reasons justify suspension (such as economic hardship). The affected agency will terminate collection of the debt if it is paid in full or discharged.

Where can the officials of the Treasury offset program take money?

You will note that some of the following are also included in the list related to the federal offset program. The following is a sample list of the sources from which the Department of the Treasury can take your money:

a) Wages, including military pay

b) Retirement benefits (i.e., pension payments)

c) Payments to government contractors and vendors

d) Travel advances and reimbursements

e) Social Security or Railroad Retirement benefits

f) Other federal payments, not specifically exempt by law

I have included a list of cases and other payments that are exempt from the long tentacles of this program in the appendix.

Now, how do you stop an offset? Pay the debt. You can do this online at pay.gov/paygov/paymydebt, by phone @888-826-3127, or by mail. The mailing address is:

Department of the Treasury

P.O. Box 979101

St. Louis, MO 63197

What kind of debts can be offset with TOP?

Well, I mentioned previously that prior federal and state taxes can be offset by current and future refunds, wage garnishments, etc. I also mentioned that child support and federal student loans can be offset from the sources mentioned. There is one other debt that most people do not realize can be a part of this offset.

If you get laid off from a job and make a successful unemployment compensation claim (or "re-employment" as it is called in Florida) the state will start paying you every month.

What happens when you get a job and just so happen forget (hopefully, not willfully) to tell the state, thereby still collecting while working? When the state finds out (as your name and social security number are reported on your employer's quarterly tax return), they will want you to pay it back. If you ignore the state, they, too, will request\certify that the federal government add your debt to the Treasury Offset Program.

So let's talk more about some of these sources of offset income.

The U.S. Department of Treasury Offset Program collects past due child support payments from the tax refunds of parents who have been court-ordered to pay child support. The program is a cooperative effort between the federal office of Child Support Enforcement (OCSE), the Internal Revenue Service, the Financial Management Service of the U.S. Department of the Treasury (remember that the Bureau of Fiscal Services, an agency within the U.S. Department of the Treasury, issues checks on behalf of other federal agencies) and the various state's child support enforcement agencies. For example, in Florida (my home state), the state's Department of Revenue is responsible for the collection of child support. However, in Hawaii, it is the Office of the Attorney General.

Under the offset program, tax refunds owed to the non-custodial parent (the parent that owes child support to the other parent) is intercepted and sent to the state's child support agency through the OCSE. In a family, the non-custodial parent is the parent the children live with less than half the time.

There are instances where the custodial parent can pay child support to the other. This can occur if the custodial parent earns a lot more than the other and lives in a much more expensive home than the other, who can only afford a home in a "bad part of town" or cannot afford a home with a separate bedroom for the children, for example. Thus, the custodial parent may have to pay child support so that the other parent can afford a better home for the health, welfare, and security of the children.

Also, please do not confuse (as many do) joint custody with custodial and non-custodial parents. These are two very different concepts and should be discussed with an attorney or with your favorite tax professional, such as an Enrolled Agent. Also, this applies to parents: You may have noticed that I never said husband, wife, or spouse. Being married is not a consideration when it comes to child support.

By the way, you need to be aware that some states charge a fee, not to exceed $25 per payment, for handling these problems.

Cases eligible for the offset program are those with a past due child support obligation. Another name for this is "arrearage." You may know of a situation where the payee of child support is subject to a wage garnishment in which they are not behind. In other words, their obligation is current. This can be negotiated and judicially enforced. It has nothing to do, necessarily, with past due amounts, but it could.

If the child support order includes an order for spousal support, the tax refund withheld may also include past due spousal support.

For situations that involve Temporary Assistance for Needy Families (TANF), the parent who is in arrears must be at least three months behind and must owe at least $150. In non-TANF cases, the amount owed must be at least $500.

When the paying parent is delinquent in their obligations and the case is certified as meeting the criteria, they will receive a "**Pre-Offset Notice**" that explains the process. This notice also includes the amount that is past due at the time of the notice. It is not unlike the IRS notice that may or may not include other years' activity or recent payments (that may have "crossed in the mail"). Rest assured, the state child support enforcement agency will update the database, but they may or may not issue a revised notice.

The notice will also include information about the administrative offset and the Passport Denial programs. These programs go beyond the scope of this book, but suffice it to say, if you owe over $51,000, the IRS will notify Homeland Security and the state, which will deny you a renewal or issuance of a passport. As such, if you are a world traveler for business or leisure, you may not be allowed to continue doing this until your taxes are taken care of.

But I digress,... back to the reason for this book.

Even if the TOP grants permission for an offset, you have the right to dispute the past due amount, and the notice I mentioned above tells you how to do just that. I have provided a sample of this three-page notice, "Notice of Intent to Offset," in the appendix.

When a tax overpayment is processed, those who have past due amounts are identified. If a refund is due, all or part of the refund is held back and sent to the office of Child Support Enforcement, then to the state's support agency (i.e., Florida's Department of the Revenue) to offset the past due amount.

At the time that the refund is offset, the U.S. Department of the Treasury's Financial Management Service sends out their own notice that the refund has been withheld to offset the past due support obligations. This notice also advises the debtor to contact the state agency. Remember, they are the ones that submitted the request to withhold any expected refunds in the first place. Calling the IRS or other government agency will not help resolve the problem, as they are just following procedures.

Since the notice does provide explicit instructions as to how to protest the offset, it is best to follow those instructions to the letter. It will save time and much aggravation later. I am not saying that a simple phone call won't resolve the problem, but you will not get anywhere without following their instructions. You do have time, as it takes three to five weeks from the time the notice of offset is issued until the U.S. Department of the Treasury's Financial Management Service actually sends the money to the state. However, the sooner the better.

Can your salary be garnished when there is a child support debt owed? The answer is a resounding **YES**! In my many years of handling payroll for my clients, I have seen this happen many times. The program is required to provide a written notice to the employee at least 30 calendar days prior to the beginning of the offset. The notice must include the following:

a) The nature, origin, and amount of the debt determined by the agency to be due;

b) The intention to collect this debt through deductions from the employee's current disposable pay account;

c) The frequency and amount stated as a fixed amount or as a percentage of pay, not to exceed 15% of the employee's disposable income;

d) A notification to the employee that the offset will continue until the debt is paid;

e) An explanation stating the policy concerning interest, penalties, and administrative costs connected to the garnishment.

f) A statement that the employee has a right to inspect and copy the program's records as it pertains to this debt;

g) A notification that the employee has the opportunity to, under agreeable terms to the program officials, enter into a written and properly structured payment plan;

h) A notification that the employee has a right to appeal the offset via a hearing with a program hearing official at the earliest possible date, but not later than 60 days after the request for the hearing was filed. However, under some circumstances, the 60 days can be extended. The hearing official is not under the control of the agency;

i) The method and time period for petitioning for a hearing;

j) A notification which states that, if a hearing is requested, the decision of the program's hearing official is final;

k) An indication that penalties that can be assessed for providing for false statements;

l) The rights and remedies available to the employee;

m) An indication that the employer has a right to refund any money withheld due to the salary offset when the offset is waived or found to be incorrect;

n) The specific mailing address to which all correspondence is to be sent. Like almost everything regarding government agencies, federal or state, sending anything to an address not prepared for what is being sent can delay their actions, sometimes in terms of months.

If you have multiple support obligations in more than one state, each state agency will ask for their own certification from the U.S.

Department of the Treasury. Once these are approved, each state will send out their own notices and the debtor will have to decide which one (or ones of them) to appeal. As you can imagine, this can get very troublesome, not to say embarrassing, if any are in error, or if your employer gets multiple orders.

An interesting question comes up when, in the case of past due child support, the child(ren) is/are no longer minor(s). For non-Temporary Assistance for Needy Families (TANF) past due amounts, once the dependent is no longer a minor, the past due amounts related to that individual child cannot be submitted for offset, even if the past due amount relates to the time when the child was a minor.

CHAPTER 12

Student Loans: Just When You Thought That You Could Get a Break...

Let us say that you have past due federal or state tax debts, have no dependent children (that you know of), and have never collected unemployment (or re-employment) benefits, and have never been married or made promises of perpetual support.

Now, you have your Enrolled Agent or CPA (attorneys generally do not prepare income tax returns for the mass market) prepares your tax return, and it shows a nice overpayment for the first time in many years. It is a refund that you desperately need.

You now get one of these notices, stating that it will be offset. You cannot understand this, as you do not owe anybody any money, except maybe the issuer of your credit card, which the expected refund will pay off.

You rack your brain, trying to understand why they are taking your money (of course, without reading the whole notice). Then you figure out that you had a federally backed student loan that was never paid. After many years it is generally forgotten, at least *you* forgot about it – or ignored it, thinking that you'll deal with it when they come after you.

Well, they are coming after you. In fact, they have tried, but since you never had a tax overpayment (state or federal), there was nothing to offset. Well, now there is.

So, what happens?

Since you took the money from a bank, you may wonder why the federal or state governments are getting involved. Maybe it is because your loan was a federally-guaranteed student loan.

When you defaulted on the note, the bank went back to the federal government, typically the U.S. Department of Education, and received their money (though maybe not all of it). As such, you are now on the hook to the federal government, again. In particular, you are on the hook with the U.S. Department of Education.

Therefore, the U.S. Department of Education will ask for this past due debt to be certified, and, once that is done, the overpayment will be used to offset some of the debt.

I will also go out on a limb and say that it will not pay off *all* of the debt, which will now include additional interest, penalties, and administrative costs. Unfortunately, once your boat starts taking on water, more can rush in on top of it… until you plug the hole.

Usually, if you are in arrears (another way to say past due), for 270 days (about nine months), AND you make no other arrangements to pay, you will need to contract the creditor, which is now the U.S. Department of Education. If you start to repay the debt and remain current (so that you are making current payments plus paying down some of the past due amount), chances are that nothing will happen to that much-needed tax refund. However, in my experience, most former students are a lot farther past due than nine months.

This is just a warning to those that have these type of student loans and stop paying (or never started) due to whatever financial high water you found yourself in. I know one student that never made even one payment on his law school debt from almost 30 years ago. (He also never worked a day as a lawyer, as he did pass a state bar exam). Because of this, he and his wife never saw a tax refund – when there was a refund to be had. There were times when he was eligible for certain refundable tax credits (i.e., earned income tax credit); however, he never saw that either.

As with a delinquent child support obligation, an initial certification must be ordered in order for the Treasury to offset the overpayment (remember this can also be a monetary credit to next year's taxes, not just a request for a refund). This is usually done in the fall of each year, several months before the "unextended" tax return is completed or even started. The debtor (that's you) will get a notice from the creditor (again, the U.S. Department of Education) letting you know that they are submitting your loan for offset.

Of course, you have the right to appeal. The appeal process when dealing with the US Department of Education, or any other US agency is very different than appealing an Internal Revenue Service decision. Special care and expertise must be taken when dealing with each agecy.

What are some of the reasons you can use when making an appeal? They are as follows (please note that this is not an exclusive list):

1. The debt has already been paid in full.

2. The loan should have been placed on default.

3. The school was closed or failed to certify the loan.

4. The borrower is deceased.

5. The borrower is permanently disabled.

6. The loan should have been refunded by the school.

7. The loan is not yours due to identity theft.

8. The loan was discharged in bankruptcy.

You must file a valid appeal within 65 days of the date of the notice. If you wish to review the file, you must make the request within 20 days, and then you must request an appeal 15 days from the date of that request. These requests must be made with the original creditor (i.e., the bank), not the U.S. Department of Education, and not any other government agency. However, you need to realize that these things have quick deadlines that must be adhered to.

Once your account has been certified for offset and there is no successful appeal, the offset remains in place until the debt is resolved via an approved written payment plan, paid in full, or consolidated into another debt.

As I explained in the child support section, not only can refunds be used to offset past-due student loan debt, but you can also be subject to wage and other income garnishments. Other income can include social security benefits (other than supplemental social security), some federal bond payments, as well as federal retirement benefits. Federal student loan garnishments apply to federal employees, including military personal.

In some situations, especially as it relates to social security benefits, you can claim a financial hardship once the offset is made, via a formal appeal to the original creditor. Financial hardship means that these benefits are your only means of support and losing them would prevent you from meeting your basic living expenses (in other words, a minimal standard of living). Of course, as with claiming this type of appeal for a federal tax debt, you will have to fully prove this fact.

Unlike a federal tax debt, where the Internal Revenue Service generally has 10 years to collect a tax debt (remember, I mentioned the Collection Stature Expiration Date, or CSED, earlier in this book, which is 10 years from when the tax was assessed), there is no statute of limitations when it comes to a student loan.

Do you recall the former law school student I mentioned earlier in this section? His debt was almost 40 years old at the time of this writing and he has no plans on paying it back. He just tries to avoid having an overpayment (refund) on his tax return and makes his payment on April 15 (maybe... but that is for another time and another book).

As with this former law school student, you will have to live with this for the rest of your life, and you will never see another tax refund. Thus, working with an experienced tax professional like an Enrolled Agent can help you plan so that you keep more at the end of the day, although any ethical tax professional will never tell you to not pay your federal obligations, tax debt, student loan, or otherwise.

Obviously, the easiest way to stop future offsets is to be current with your obligations. It is also fair to say that life gets in the way. However, once your loan is in default, you need to get it out of default. Then, and only then, will there not be any offset.

It is not uncommon for students to take out loans from several sources (i.e., undergraduate, graduate, and postgraduate loans). It is also not uncommon for former students, overwhelmed with ever-rising financial waters, to not only stop paying on one loan, but to stop paying on *all* of them. After all, if you have more than one loan, total monthly payments can sink your financial ship.

As I mentioned before, you can consolidate different loans into one, which may reduce your monthly payment. You cannot do this on your own, so you will need to make formal arrangements with the creditors. You can also make other payment plans with your creditors. This is sometimes called "rehabilitating the loan." Rehabilitating a loan is like modifying your mortgage obligations with the bank that holds the note. "Mr. Google" has a lot of information on this subject.

Neither consolidation or rehabilitation is an immediate process. However, consolidation is generally faster.

If you need to be bailed out of a dire financial situation, don't wait. Once an offset or a wage garnishment is in place, consolidation is not available right away. Your rescue window has closed... the offset remains in place until the debt is paid and/or no longer in default.

There can be a life preserver here if there's a tax refund coming, you may be able to employ some strategic planning. File an extension of your income tax returns (with the appropriate amount tax paid) until the student loan is out of default. When the loan is out of default, your refund is safe from the offset. Seek help from a tax professional (you get the common theme, here?) like an

Enrolled Agent so that he or she can help you traverse through the tricky waters of tax returns, extensions and the refund process.

If you are seeking a discharge of the debt (again, look to "Mr. Google" for assistance), you will need to apply for the discharge. This can provide a respite from the federal offset while you are going through this process. However, as with many government agencies, the offset for a current refund may still happen while you wait for a decision. In fact, you may want to file for an extension on that tax return, because you might just save your boat from sinking and save that refund after all.

Federal student loans can be cancelled in certain circumstances. There are limited federal student loan cancellation programs, also known as discharge or forgiveness programs, for federal student loan borrowers. See the chart below for a list of these programs:

Type of Forgiveness, Cancellation, or Discharge	Direct Loans	Federal Family Education Loan (FFEL) Program Loans	Perkins Loans
Public Service Loan Forgiveness	X	X*	X*
Teacher Loan Forgiveness	X	X	
Perkins Loan Cancellation (includes Teacher Cancellation)			X
Total and Permanent Disability Discharge	X	X	X
Death Discharge	X	X	X
Bankruptcy Discharge (in rare cases)	X	X	X
Closed School Discharge	X	X	X
False Certification of Student Eligibility or Unauthorized Signature/Unauthorized Payment Discharge	X	X	
Unpaid Refund Discharge	X	X	

*FFEL Program loans and Perkins Loans may become eligible for Public Service Loan Forgiveness if they are consolidated into the Direct Loan Program.

You may also "raise defenses to repayment," also known as borrower defenses. You may qualify regardless of whether your loan is current or in default. You are entitled to these cancellations by law, but you must meet very specific requirements to get this comprehensive relief. A successful cancellation not only makes the loan obligation go away, but, in most cases, the government must also give back any payments you have made (whether voluntarily or involuntarily) and help clean up your credit. This is the most complete relief you can get.

Because the relief is so broad, there are very specific conditions you must meet to get these cancellations. It is a good idea to go through the list and see if any apply to your situation. You must fill out an application form if you apply for a cancellation, as well as meet the specific conditions for the specific cancellation program you are applying for.

The federal loan cancellation programs described here are available outside of the bankruptcy process. You can also cancel your federal loan in bankruptcy. This is a difficult process, but not impossible. You must prove "undue hardship" in bankruptcy court to get a bankruptcy discharge of your federal loan.

There may be tax consequences associated with some of these cancellation programs. Loan amounts cancelled through the job-related or school-related cancellation programs should not be considered taxable income. Other cancellations may be taxable income. However, you may not have to pay taxes. For example, you may be able to claim insolvency status using I.R.S. Form 982. It is a good idea to consult a tax professional like an Enrolled Agent for more information.

The appendix of this book includes several applications (see the list below). These and others can be found on the Student Loan Borrowers Assistance Project website. The link for the forms is https://www.studentloanborrowerassistance.org/resources/refe rral-resource/important-forms/

- Borrower Defense Application

- School Closure Loan Discharge

- Direct Loan Consolidation Application

- Disability Discharge Forms

- Economic Hardship Deferment

Another question that affected individuals should concern themselves with are the tax consequences of a discharged or student loan. Generally, under Federal law, everything is taxable, from whatever source derived (Internal Revenue Code Section 61) unless it is specifically exempt (think Al Capone).

Why am I telling you this? Because the cancellation of a debt is income to you, unless it meets some of the allowable exclusions criteria. In addition to mortgage interest and credit card debts, cancellation of a student loan is also included in what is considered income.

So, what are some of the exemptions? One has to refer to Internal Revenue Code §108 for this. In addition, the IRS created a separate form, 982, when the real estate market tanked, starting in 2007. This form tells the IRS whether any cancellation of debt can be excluded from income.

If you file bankruptcy, having to include these discharged amounts in your income seems like a double hit. First, you file bankruptcy, then, you get hit with income and an increased tax bill. Doesn't sound fair, does it? Well, the Internal Revenue Code has a provision to exclude this. It has another if you are deemed insolvent. This is more of a legal concept than a tax, but basically it means that your liabilities (the money you owed) exceed the amount of your assets (the fair market value of the items you own, including retirement accounts). We are not talking about creditor-protected items, like some retirement plans, just what is taxable and what can be excluded.

Student loan cancellations, however, are included in your income. This means the student (or former student) will have to include the amount in their income calculations, unless it is excluded under IRC §108. These can amount to anywhere from tens to hundreds of thousands of dollars. You need to include the discharge as income in the year that the creditor declares the debt uncollectible. They will issue and send a form to you, the 1099-C, Cancellation of Debt.

Following is copy of the form.

As you can see from this copy, the note includes the debtor's name and social security number, or, when a business is involved, its federal employee identification number (FEIN). This form requires that the following information be included: the name and FEIN of the person to whom the credit was given, the date the debt was cancelled, the amount discharged, and a description of the debt.

In addition to causing a large income tax problem for you, it can cause other tax issues as well. First, it can put you into a higher tax bracket. Remember, we have a progressive tax system, meaning that the higher your taxable income is, the higher your tax rate.

Below is a chart of 2018 tax rates under the Tax Cuts and Jobs Act that was passed in December 2017.

Tax Rate	2018 Filing Status & Taxable Income Range				
	Single	Married Filing Jointly & Surviving Spouse	Married Filing Separate	Head of Household	Trust
10%	0-9,525	0-19,050	0-9,525	0-13,600	0-2,550
12%	9,525-38,700	19,050-77,400	9,525-38,700	13,600-51,800	NA
22%	38,700-82,500	77,400-165,000	38,700-82,500	51,800-82,500	NA
24%	82,500-157,500	165,000-315,000	82,500-157,500	82,500-157,500	2,550-9,150
32%	157,500-200,000	315,000-400,000	157,500-200,000	157,500-200,000	NA
35%	200,000-500,000	400,000-600,000	200,000-300,000	200,000-500,000	9,150-12,500
37%	500,000+	600,000+	300,000+	500,000+	12,500+

Depending on the amount of the debt and your other income, the tax can be as high as 37% of the cancelled amount.

In March 2010, Congress passed the Patient Protection and Affordable Care Act (PPACA). Most of the general public are aware of the Affordable Care Act (commonly known as "Obamacare") because it had to do with health insurance.

However, what many people don't know is that it also included a new tax called the Net Investment Income Tax ("NIIT"), which became effective January 1, 2013. The NIIT applies a tax rate of 3.8% to certain net investment income (interest, dividends, net capital gains, etc.) of individuals, estates and trusts that have income above a certain amount. Individuals will owe the tax if they have net investment income and have modified adjusted gross income over the following thresholds:

Filing Status	Threshold Amount
Married filing jointly	$250,000
Married filing separately	$125,000
Single	$200,000
Head of household (with qualifying person)	$200,000
Qualifying widow(er) with dependent child	$250,000

In addition, not only does your taxable income go up, so does your adjusted gross income.

What is the difference between these two?

You first compute adjusted gross income which is the total of ALL of your income less some "adjustments." Taxable income is your adjusted gross income (AGI) less your exemptions (prior to 2018) and your itemized or standard deductions. As such, when you have to include cancellation of debt along with the rest of your income, the adjusted gross income goes up. Well, including the extra income it can have a bigger impact on your taxes.

Take, for example, the itemized deduction for medical expenses. Your medical expenses have to exceed 7.5% of AGI in order for you to claim the deduction. Let's say you have a student debt cancellation of $100,000. This increases your AGI by $100,000, and so now the amount of your medical expenses has to exceed $7,500 more than it would if you did not have cancellation of debt income ($100,000 x 7.5%).

Let us talk about social security next. If you are receiving these retirement benefits, your "regular" income may be low enough that none of your social security income is taxable. However, with the cancellation of debt now translating into taxable income, up to 85% of never-before-taxed social security benefits are now taxable as well.

Prior to 2017, if you were an employee, you were able to deduct business expenses that were not reimbursed by your employer. However, these expenses had to exceed 2% of your AGI in order to be deducted. If you had a student loan debt cancellation of, say, $100,000, your unreimbursed expenses now have to be $2,000 more than before the cancellation ($100,000 x 2%) in order to take the deduction.

Of course, all of this was before the passing of the Tax Cuts and Jobs Act (TCJA) which eliminated these deductions.

The same goes for casualty and theft losses, which had to exceed 10% of AGI. However, the TCJA eliminated these deductions as well, except for federally declared disaster areas. (In recent years, the IRS removed the 10% floor whenever this happens anyway).

But I digress again... my point is that the cancellation of debt has many other tax implications besides just paying higher income taxes, and, as we discussed earlier in this book, if the tax is too high and you do not pay, you can be subject to tax levies.

On the plus side, your state sales tax itemized deduction will be higher, and, if that amount is higher than your state income taxes, you get to claim the higher amount. However, as it is with all things taxes, there are exceptions to the exceptions. The TCJA put a cap on all state and local taxes (including real estate taxes). This cap is now only $10,000, so if your real estate taxes are already over $10,000, then you get no benefit from the higher state and local sales taxes.

Now let's discuss a non-tax problem. If you are over age 65, you must be on Medicare. If your income is higher than a certain threshold, your Medicare premiums will go up. In 2018, that threshold is $170,000 for married filing jointly, based on the 2017 tax return. If you are taking advantage of the subsidiaries for health insurance on health.gov, this higher income would prevent you from getting the benefit of a subsidiary. If you received a subsidiary, followed by the dreaded 1099-C letting you know that there is cancellation of debt income, AND you do not adjust the health.gov account, then you may have to pay it back. That's the full amount of the subsidiary, due when you file your return.

Now, what would a tax help guide be if it did not tell you, the reader, of yet-another exception? In addition to the changes I have already mentioned, the TCJA allowed for an exemption from the taxability of student loan cancellation income.

What is that, you may ask?

Any student loan that is cancelled due to the death of the student or "total or permanent disability" is no longer taxable. These new provisions are for discharges that take place from January 1, 2018 through and including December 31, 2025. Prior to this year, even if you experienced total and permanent disability, any student loan debt cancellation would still be considered income. And, like many provisions of the new law, it is not permanent. However, Congress can extend or reverse these provisions at any time... just as we experienced in prior years. Most recently, on February 9, 2018, Congress extended 75 expired provisions (retroactive to the beginning of 2017, I might add). So stay tuned, folks! Things change quickly on the tax seas.

As you can imagine, the old law which called for including cancellation of student loan debt in income put additional burdens on total and permanently disabled students. It disqualified them for need-based benefits such as Medicaid or Social Security Insurance Benefits that are specifically designed to help individuals with disabilities who cannot work. Typically, their income is so low they cannot pay their student loans.

For example, if you have $50,000 of debt cancelled, you can wind up owing $5,000 or more in federal taxes. Then, you have to add potential state income taxes into the mix. Now, when you cannot pay the tax bill in full, you will need to enter into a properly structured payment plan with Uncle Sam. Then, penalties and interest will be added to the tax you owe, and, when you the enlist the help of a qualified tax professional like an Enrolled Agent, the total cost gets even higher. It is a lot to consider.

You heard me use the words "discharge" and "forgiveness." They may sound like one and the same, but they are not. In the financial world, loan discharge happens only when the borrower dies or becomes totally and permanently disabled. Forgiveness, on the other hand, occurs when eligible federal student loan debt is wiped out after the borrower fills a public service job for a set number of years. Either way, the debt is gone.

CHAPTER 13

Innocent Versus Injured Spouse

I Was on the Ship but
I Didn't Know Where We Were Going

Many people, including some in the tax professional community, use these terms interchangeably. However, they are very different. The only commonality is that, when a joint tax refund is used to offset the debts of only one spouse, the other spouse may have some recourse.

The concept of "innocent spouse" comes into play when the IRS claims that more taxes are owed on a jointly filed return. Typically, both spouses are "individually and severally" liable for everything on a tax return at the time of its filing, even when all the items on it pertain to just one spouse.

Spouses are deemed responsible, even if they later abandon ship on the marriage.

Here is an example: A client came in with notices showing a mid-five figure, past-due tax balance that had been owed for several years. These debts were reported on returns filed as a single taxpayer and she did not dispute them.

In the course of planning how to pay these debts, I "pulled" the transcripts to see what the IRS had on her account, as I do for every client. What I found was a surprise.

The account transcripts showed that there were *additional* taxes owed (not including penalties and interest) for *another* six figures over several more years.

For these additional years, my client had filed a joint return. Now, the IRS wanted to have her include these debts in the payment plan we were considering.

When I questioned the client, I was told the new debts were due to the income of the other spouse, and he had promised to pay those when they divorced, as stipulated in the divorce decree. The IRS does not have to recognize this section of the decree (though they do when it comes to making an innocent spouse claim, which I'll discuss later), and will instead come after both spouses. Once my client pays this part of the overall debt, she has to sue in civil or family court to get her ex-spouse to pay her back.

So, what is my client to do? In actuality, there is nothing she can do, as she missed the timing for filing an innocent spouse claim. My hope is that this will serve as a cautionary tale for you, dear reader. Make sure you read every tax return you file jointly and ask questions if you don't understand it. If your spouse has pulled the wool over your eyes, you only have a limited time to take action and divorce yourself from your spouse's debt.

There are actually three forms of relief provided by the Internal Revenue Code (IRC). IRC Section 6015 has several subsections that deal with innocent spouse, §6015(b), §6015(c) and §6015(f). These sections allow for one spouse to claim relief from the tax debt due to the actions of another. If the "innocent" spouse did not know, or had no reason to know, of the understated income or overstated expenses or deductions, the innocent spouse can be found to be not responsible for the tax debts. The spouse seeking relief from the tax debt is called the requesting spouse.

Generally, spouses need to be separate or divorced for this to happen, depending on which subpart of the code applies, §6015(b) or §6015(c). §6015(f) is the section for equitable relief.

You must request innocent spouse relief (or separation of liability relief) within two years of the date the IRS first attempted to collect the tax from you. For equitable relief, you must request relief during the period of time the IRS can collect the tax from you (the collection statute expiration date).

If you're looking for a refund of tax you paid, then you must request it within the statutory period for seeking a refund (generally three years after the date the return is filed, or two years following the payment of the tax, whichever is later). Refunds aren't available under separation of liability relief.

An innocent spouse request is filed on Federal form 8857. You'll find a copy of this form in the appendix.

The subsections of §6015 are briefly described below:

Innocent Spouse Relief provides relief from additional tax if your spouse or former spouse failed to report income, reported income improperly, or claimed improper deductions or credits.

You must meet **all** of the following conditions to qualify for innocent spouse relief:

- You filed a joint return that has an understatement of tax (deficiency) that's solely attributable to your spouse's "erroneous item." An erroneous item includes income received by your spouse but omitted from the joint return. Deductions, credits, and property basis amounts are also erroneous items if they're incorrectly reported on the joint return, and

- You establish that at the time you signed the joint return you didn't know, and had no reason to know, that there was an understatement of tax, and

- Taking into account all the facts and circumstances, it would be unfair to hold you liable for the understatement of tax.

Separation of Liability Relief provides for the separate allocation of additional tax owed between you and your former spouse, or your current spouse you're legally separated from or not living with, when an item wasn't reported properly on a joint return. You'll only be responsible for the amount of tax allocated to you.

To qualify for separation of liability relief, you must have filed a joint return and meet **one** of the following requirements at the time you request relief:

- You're divorced or legally separated from the spouse with whom you filed the joint return, or

- You're widowed, or

- You haven't been a member of the same household as the spouse with whom you filed the joint return at any time during the previous 12 months, ending on the date you request relief.

If you had knowledge of the item that caused your taxes to be understated when you signed the joint return, you don't qualify for separation of liability relief.

Equitable Relief may apply when you don't qualify for either innocent spouse or separation of liability relief for something not reported properly on a joint return and generally attributable to your spouse. You may also qualify for equitable relief if the amount of tax reported is correct on your joint return, but the tax wasn't paid with the return.

- If you don't qualify for innocent spouse relief or separation of liability relief, you may still qualify for equitable relief. To qualify for equitable relief, you must establish that under all the facts and circumstances, it would be unfair to hold you liable for the understatement or underpayment of tax.

- The IRS will take into account physical and emotional abuse, as well as financial control of the non-requesting spouse, when determining if equitable relief is warranted.

Exception for Equitable Relief

The amount of time you have to request equitable relief depends on whether you are seeking relief from a balance due, seeking a credit or refund, or both.

Balance Due

Generally, you must file your request within the time period the IRS has to collect the tax. The IRS typically has 10 years from the date the tax liability was assessed to collect the tax. In certain cases, the 10-year period is suspended. The amount of time the suspension is in effect will extend the time the IRS has to collect the tax. See Pub. 594, The IRS Collection Process, for more details.

Credit or Refund

Generally, you must file your request within three years from the date the original return was filed, or within two years from the date the tax was paid, whichever is later. But you may have more time to file if you live in a federally declared disaster area or you are physically or mentally unable to manage your financial affairs. See Pub. 556, Examination of Returns, Appeal Rights, and Claims for Refund, for more details.

Both a Balance Due and a Credit or Refund

If you are seeking a refund of amounts you paid and relief from a balance due over and above what you have paid, the time period for filing for a credit or refund will apply to any payments you have made, and the time period for collection of a balance due amount will apply to any unpaid liability.

Form 8857 Filed by or on Behalf of a Decedent

An executor (including any other duly appointed representative) may pursue a Form 8857 filed during the decedent's lifetime. An executor may also file Form 8857 as long as the decedent satisfied the eligibility requirements while alive. For purposes of separation of liability relief (which will be discussed later), the decedent's marital status is determined on the date relief was requested or the date of death, whichever is earlier.

Situations in Which You Are Not Entitled to Relief

You are not entitled to innocent spouse relief for any tax year in which any of the following situations applied:

1. In a final decision, a court considered whether to grant you relief from joint liability and decided not to do so.

2. In a final decision, a court did not consider whether to grant you relief from joint liability, but you meaningfully participated in the proceeding and could have asked for relief.

3. You entered into an offer in compromise with the IRS.

4. You entered into a closing agreement with the IRS that disposed of the same liability for which you want to seek relief.

By law, the IRS must contact your spouse (or former spouse). In this situation, the spouse is called the Intervenor. There are no exceptions, even for victims of spousal abuse or domestic violence.

The IRS will inform your spouse (or former spouse) that you filed Form 8857 and will allow him or her to participate in the process. If you are requesting relief from joint and several liability on a joint return, the IRS must also inform him or her of its preliminary and final determinations regarding your request for relief.

To protect your privacy, the IRS will not disclose your personal information (such as your current name, address, phone number(s), or information about your employer, your income, or your assets). However, any other information you provide that the IRS uses to make a determination about your request could be disclosed to the person you list on Form 8857, line 5. If you have concerns about your privacy or the privacy of others, you should redact (or black out) personal information in the material you submit.

Factors the IRS considers in determining whether you had reason to know of either an understated tax or that your spouse (or former spouse) could or would pay the reported tax liability include, but are not limited to the following:

- Your level of education.

- Any deceit or evasiveness on the part of your spouse (or former spouse).

- Your degree of involvement in the activity that generated the income tax debt.

- Your involvement in business or household financial matters.

- Your business or financial expertise.

- Any lavish or unusual expenditures compared with past spending levels.

Abuse by your Spouse (or Former Spouse)

If you can prove that you were the victim of abuse (not including verbal threats), then this may tip the scales in your favor. Abuse comes in many forms and can include physical, psychological, sexual, or emotional abuse. It can include efforts to control, isolate, humiliate, and intimidate you, or undermine your ability to reason independently and be able to do what is required under the tax laws. The IRS will consider all the facts and circumstances in determining whether you were abused.

The IRS also will consider the impact of your spouse's (or former spouse's) alcohol or drug abuse in determining whether you were abused. The IRS may even find that the abuse of your child or other family member living in the household may constitute abuse of you.

Legal Obligations

The IRS will consider whether you or your spouse (or former spouse) has a legal obligation to pay the outstanding federal income tax debt. A legal obligation in this case would be an obligation arising from a divorce decree (or other legally binding agreement).

This factor will weigh in favor of relief if your former spouse has the sole legal obligation to pay the outstanding income tax liability as spelled out in your divorce decree or agreement.

This factor will be neutral if you knew, or had reason to know, when entering into the divorce decree or agreement, that your former spouse would not pay the income tax liability.

This factor will weigh against relief if you have the sole legal obligation. Even if your spouse or former spouse has declared bankruptcy and had the tax debt discharged, it does not matter. This fact will not be considered in determining whether you are solely responsible for the debt.

This factor will be neutral if, based on an agreement or consent order, both spouses have a legal obligation to pay the outstanding income tax liability, the spouses are not separated or divorced, or the divorce decree or agreement is silent as to any obligation to pay the outstanding income tax liability.

Significant Benefit

The IRS will consider whether you significantly benefited from the unpaid income tax liability or understated tax.

A "significant benefit" is any benefit beyond what you would normally be expect in terms of financial support.

For example, if you enjoyed the benefits of a lavish lifestyle, such as owning luxury assets and taking expensive vacations, this factor will weigh against you in your request for relief. If, however, your spouse (or former spouse) controlled the household and business finances, or there was abuse (as mentioned earlier), and he or she made the decision on spending funds for a lavish lifestyle, then this mitigates this factor so that it is neutral.

If only your spouse (or former spouse) significantly benefitted from the unpaid tax or understatement, and you had little or no benefit, or your spouse (or former spouse) enjoyed the benefit to your detriment, this factor will weigh in favor of relief.

If the amount of unpaid or understated tax was small, so that neither spouse received a significant benefit, then this factor is neutral. Whether the amount of unpaid or understated tax is so small that neither you nor your spouse received a significant benefit will vary depending on the facts and circumstances of each case.

Compliance with Income Tax Laws

The IRS will also consider whether you have made a good faith effort to comply with the income tax laws in the tax years that following the ones covered by your request for relief.

If you are compliant for the tax years that follow your divorce, then this factor will weigh in your favor. If you are not compliant, then this factor will weigh against relief. If you made a good faith effort to comply with the tax laws but were unable to fully comply, then this factor will be neutral. For example, if you filed an income tax return on time but couldn't pay your taxes in full due to a poor financial or economic situation after the divorce, then this factor will be neutral.

If you remain married to your spouse, whether or not you are legally separated or living apart, and continue to file joint returns after requesting relief, then this factor will be neutral as long as the joint returns are compliant with the tax laws. If not, then this factor will weigh against relief.

If you remain married to your spouse but file separate returns, this factor will weigh in favor of relief, if, again, you are compliant with the tax laws. If not, then this factor will weigh against relief. If you made a good faith effort to comply with the tax laws but were unable to fully comply, then this factor will be neutral. For example, if you filed your tax return on time but were unable to fully pay the tax liability due to a poor financial or economic situation as a result of being separated or living apart from your spouse, then this factor will be neutral.

Mental or Physical Health

The IRS will consider whether you were in poor physical or mental health. This factor will weigh in favor of relief if you were in poor mental or physical health at one of the following times:

1. At the time the return or returns for which the request for relief relates were filed.

2. At the time you reasonably believed the return or returns were filed.

3. At the time you request relief.

The IRS will consider the nature, extent, and duration of your condition, including the ongoing economic impact of your illness. If you were in neither poor physical nor poor mental health, this factor is neutral.

Let me give you an example of "had not known or had no reason to know." This can be shown in a recent tax court case. One spouse had a big gambling problem with very large losses. To pay off the gambling debt to the casinos, the gambling spouse took a rather large distribution from a 401K plan. To make matters worse, it was the spouse's 401K and the gambler forged his spouse's signature. The administrator of the 401K sent the account owner a form 1099R, indicating the distribution. However, the gambler intercepted the form. When they filed the return, this distribution was never included.

The couple later received a CP2000, which if you read my first book, *Now What? I Got A Notice from the IRS. Help!*, you would know that this is an IRS notice that states that the IRS has items on your account that you did not report on your return. This notice indicated that the couple owed a rather large tax debt, as well as a 10% penalty for early withdrawal, as she was under 59½. Again, the gambler intercepted this letter.

Subsequently, the couple divorced, and it was not until the non-gambling spouse received a threatening letter stating that there was unpaid tax did she realize what her ex-husband did not do. This spouse filed an Innocent Spouse claim and the IRS denied it. Since the spouse did not know of the gambling addiction, nor did she know about the losses or the withdrawal, the United States Tax Court agreed that this spouse was indeed innocent and did not owe the tax. The gambling spouse did not dispute this before the court. The court agreed that the innocent spouse did not know about the distribution (forged signature) and did not benefit from it (it paid off the gambling debts of the other spouse).

Though this case seems cut and dried, it is not always this way, especially when the Intervenor disputes the claim of the other ("S/He knew about this and benefitted from it," for example). So, of course, it is strongly recommended that, if you want to seek relief under this section, you get competent, experienced assistance from an Enrolled Agent, CPA or lawyer. Most of these claims do not go to tax court.

Now that we briefly discussed innocent spouse, let's see what the difference is with Injured Spouse.

An injured spouse claim is for allocation of a joint refund, while innocent spouse is for relief or allocation on a joint and several liability (basically, joint liability) of a joint return. You're an injured spouse if all or part of your share of a refund from a joint return was or will be applied against separate past-due federal tax, state tax, child or spousal support, or federal non-tax debt (such as a student loan) owed by your spouse. If you're an injured spouse, you may be entitled to recoup your share of the refund. Generally, it is a pure mathematical calculation.

This section is important to understand because of the effect of the Federal Offset program. As we discussed, if you owe a joint tax debt, the IRS will take a future refund (the offset). If you filed a joint return and you're not responsible for your spouse's debt, you're entitled to request your portion of the refund back from the IRS. You may file a claim for this amount by filing Form 8379, Injured Spouse Allocation (a copy is in the appendix.)

You may file Form 8379 in any of the following ways:

- With your original joint tax return (Form 1040, Form 1040A, or Form 1040EZ),

- With your amended joint tax return (Form 1040X), or

- By itself after you receive notification of an offset.

The IRS can process your Form 8379 before an offset occurs. If you file Form 8379 with your original return, it may take up to 11 weeks to process an electronically-filed return, or 14 weeks if you filed a paper return. If you file the Form 8379 by itself after a joint return has been processed, then processing will take about eight weeks.

As the form states in its title, the Injured Spouse claim is an allocation. The allocation would be on the following items between the spouses:

- W-2 Income

- Other Income

- Adjustments to Income

- Standard or Itemized Deductions

- Exemptions

- Credits, except the Earned Income Tax Credit

- Other Taxes

- Estimated Tax Payments (federal income tax withheld is applied to the spouse from which the amount was withheld)

The Internal Revenue Service will make its determination and then refund any money owed to the injured spouse, and part of that money will be used as an offset against the other spouse's tax obligation.

CONCLUSION

Bon Voyage, Dear Readers!

This book has covered many of the things taxpayers should know about why their refund was taken and what forms of relief are out there. In any of these situations, you can deal with all of this on your own. However, just as with many facets of everyday life, the more complicated the matter, the more you may need professional assistance.

Remember, the many agencies of the United States Department of Treasury, especially the Internal Revenue Service, are aggressive when it comes to collecting taxes and making sure that your federally backed obligations are taken care of. They do what they have to do make sure that this happens.

The United States Department of Treasury agencies (especially the IRS) march to the drum of the United States government, their customer. An experienced tax professional – such as an Enrolled Agent, Certified Public Accountant, or an attorney – has *you* as their customer and will look out for *your* best interests.

The seas can be rough, and unless you're an expert seaman (or seawoman), your boat may sink. It's so much easier to an experienced Captain (ahem, EA, CPA or attorney) at the helm.

Thankfully, you do not have to go through any of this alone.

ABOUT THE AUTHOR AND SFS TAX PROBLEM SOLUTIONS

Jeffrey A. Schneider

Jeffrey Schneider EA, CTRS, NTPI Fellow, ACT-E has the knowledge and expertise to help you reach a favorable outcome with the IRS. Whether you need assistance with reducing the amount of your tax debt, filing a back-tax return, or preparing a tax settlement by negotiating offers in compromise and filing installment agreements.

As an Enrolled Agent, Jeffrey Schneider is one of America's Tax Experts®, who has earned the privilege of representing taxpayers before all administrative levels of the Internal Revenue Service.

He is a Fellow of the National Tax Practice Institute (NTPI), a Past President of the Florida Society of Enrolled Agents, a former member of the Palm Beach Chapter and Treasure Coast Chapter of the Florida Society of Enrolled Agents, and a past Director on the Board of the National Association of Enrolled Agents (NAEA).

He is a frequent speaker at many other tax organizations around the country as well as other public speaking forums on tax and time management. He also has led many webinars on all areas of tax.

SFS Tax Problem Solutions

We have provided tax and accounting services for almost 40 years to taxpayers just like you. SFS Tax Problem Solutions has saved their clients hundreds of thousands of dollars over the years. Whether you need help with IRS or state audits, offers in compromise, appeals, collections, penalties and interest abatement, IRS tax liens and levies, wage garnishments, delinquent taxes, or tax preparation, we have the expertise and experience to resolve all your tax problems.

Stay Connected with Jeffrey A. Schneider

http://nowwhathelp.com

http://sfstaxproblemsolutions.com/

http://igotataxnotice.com

Email: info@sfstaxacct.com

APPENDIX

Now What About Some Examples?

SAMPLE LETTER - NOTICE OF INTENT TO OFFSET

(Enter Date Letter Mailed)

(Enter Name of Debtor)

(Enter Address of Debtor)

RE: Amt. of past due debt owed to: (Enter IWV.R/VQ Fund Name) $ (Enter the Amount owed)

Date debt became past due: (Enter Date of Delinquency) Account/ Case Number: (Enter Internal Number if Used)

Dear: (Enter the Name of Debtor)

You have not paid the amount you owe to (Enter MWR/VQ Fund Name) .

(If not previously provided, explain the nature of the debt, for example, bounced check #XX dated XX/XX/XX). If you do not pay your debt or take other action described below before (Enter the date equal to 60 days from the date of this letter), (Enter PIVVR/VQ Fund Name) will submit your debt to the US Dept of Treasury

Offset Program. The total amount listed above includes a service charge of $ (Enter the amount of your service charge).

TREASURY OFFSET PROGRAM (TOP): Once your debt is submitted to the TOP, the U.S. Department of the Treasury (U.S. Treasury) will reduce or withhold any of your eligible Federal payments by the amount of your debt. This process, known as "offset" is authorized by the Debt Collection Act of 1982 and the Debt Collection Improvement Act of 1996. You may not receive another notice before your payment is offset. Federal payments eligible for offset include:

1. Your income tax refunds (See Attachment A for additional information);

2. Your Federal Salary pay, including military pay (See Attachment A for additional information);

3. Your Federal retirement, including military retirement pay;

4. Your contractor/ vendor payments;

5. Certain Federal benefit payments, such as Social Security

    {other than Supplemental Security Income (SSI)}, Railroad Retirement (other than tier 2), and Black Lung (part B) benefits; and

6. Other Federal payments, including certain loans to you, that are not exempt from offset.

Before we submit your debt to the TOP, we are required to tell you that you may (1) inspect and copy our records related to your debt;

(2) request a review of our determination that you owe this debt and if required by law, request a waiver of all or a part of the debt; this review may be in the form of a hearing if we determine that a hearing is required; and (3) enter into an acceptable written repayment agreement. (See Attachment A for additional information).

TO AVOID THE TOP, you must do one of the following by (Enter the date equal to 60 days from the date of this letter):

1. REPAY YOUR DEBT: To repay your debt, send a check or money order, payable to (Enter the name of your MWR/VQ Fund) for the full amount that you owe to: (Enter your Fund's mailing address.)

2. AGREE TO A REPAYMENT PLAN: If you are unable to pay your debt in full, you must contact (Enter the name of the MWR/VQ Fund POC and telephone number) , agree to a repayment plan acceptable to us, and make payments required in the repayment plan.

3. REQUEST A REVIEW IF YOU BELIEVE THE DEBT IS NOT OWED: If you believe that all or a part of the debt is not past due or legally enforceable, you must send evidence to support your position to: (Enter the name and address of local MWR/VQ Fund) We will inform you of our decision about your debt.

BANKRUPTCY: If you filed for bankruptcy and the automatic bankruptcy stay is in effect, you are not subject to offset while the stay is in effect. Please notify us of the stay by sending evidence concerning the bankruptcy.

If you make or provide any knowingly false or frivolous statements, representations, or evidence, you may be liable for penalties under the False Claims Act (31 U.S. C. SS3729-3731), or other applicable statutes and/or criminal penalties under 18 U.S. C. SS 286, 287, 1001 and 1002, or other applicable statutes.

Unless prohibited by Law or contract, we will promptly refund to you any amounts paid by you or deducted from your payment for Enclosure (1) your debt which are later waived or found not owed to the United States.

If you have any questions about this letter or your rights, you should contact (Enter the name of the MNR/VQ Fund POC and telephone number) immediately.

Sincerely,

(Enter the name of your MWR/VQ Fund)

PAYMENTS EXEMPT BY FEDERAL LAW		
Payment Agency	**Type of Payment**	**Statutory Exemption (U.S. Code)**
Department of Agriculture	Federal Crop Insurance indemnity payments	7 U.S.C. § 1509
Department of Defense	Survivors benefits (military retirement) payments	10 U.S.C. § 1450(i)
Department of Education	Payments under a program administered by the Secretary of Education under Title IV of the Higher Education Act of 1965	31 U.S.C. § 3716(c)(1)(C)
Department of Homeland Security - Federal Emergency Management Agency	Payments made under the Cerro Grande Fire Assistance Act (covering claims resulting from the wildfire in New Mexico in May 2000)	Public Law 106-246
Department of the Interior	Payments under a program administered by the Secretary of Education under Title IV of the Higher Education Act of 1965	31 U.S.C. § 3716(c)(1)(C)
Department of Labor	Longshore and Worker's Compensation Act payments Energy Employees Occupational Illness Compensation Program Payments Federal Employees Compensation Program Payments	33 U.S.C. § 916 42 U.S.C. § 7385(a) 5 U.S.C. § 8130
Department of Labor/Social Security Administration	Payments under the Black Lung Benefits Act, other than payments under Part B	30 U.S.C. § 932(a) [incorporating 33 U.S.C. § 916]
Department of the Treasury	Payments under the tariff laws	31 U.S.C. § 3701(d)
Department of Veterans Affairs	Payments of benefits under any law administered by the Secretary of Veterans Affairs, including: * Pension programs * Parents= dependency and indemnity compensation programs * Disability and death compensation * Dependency and indemnity compensation * Monetary educational assistance * Monetary benefits under training (including work study allowances) and rehabilitation programs * Special monetary benefits * Life insurance payments * Funeral and burial expenses * Financial assistance for adapted housing and automobile equipment * Minimum income widow	38 U.S.C. § 5301(a)

161

TREASURY OFFSET PROGRAM
Payments Exempt from Offset by Disbursing Officials
(Non-tax Debt Collection)

PAYMENTS EXEMPT BY FEDERAL LAW		
Payment Agency	**Type of Payment**	**Statutory Exemption (U.S. Code)**
Department of Veterans Affairs (continued)	* Special allowance under 38 U.S.C. § 1312 * Attorney fees withheld from retroactive benefits for representation at the Board of Veterans Appeals * Clothing allowance * Apportionment funds * Accrued benefits * Child support withholdings * Reimbursements for travel, medical, rehabilitation, and health care related needs and activities	
Railroad Retirement Board	Tier 2 Railroad Retirement benefit payments	45 U.S.C. § 231m,
Social Security Administration/ Department of Health and Human Services	Payments made under the Social Security Act, except to the extent provided under 31 U.S.C. § 3716(c) [Debt Collection Improvement Act]	31 U.S.C. § 3701(d)

PAYMENTS EXEMPT BY FEDERAL LAW FOR COLLECTION OF STATE NONTAX DEBTS AND PAST-DUE SUPPORT OBLIGATIONS		
Payment Agency	**Type of Payment**	**Statutory Exemption (U.S. Code)**
See above	All payments listed above as "Payments Exempt by Federal Law"	See above
Department of Labor/Social Security Administration	Payments under the Black Lung Benefits Act	31 U.S.C. § 3716(h), 30 U.S.C. § 932(a) [incorporating 33 U.S.C. § 916]
Railroad Retirement Board	Railroad Retirement benefit payments	45 U.S.C. § 231m, 31 U.S.C. § 3716(h)
Social Security Administration	Payments made under the Social Security Act	31 U.S.C. § 3701(d), 31 U.S.C. § 3716(h), 42 U.S.C. § 407 and 42 U.S.C. § 1383(d)(1)

PAYMENTS EXEMPT BY ACTION OF THE SECRETARY OF THE TREASURY (31 U.S.C. § 3716(c)(3)(B))	
Payment Agency	**Type of Payment**
All Agencies	Federal Loan payments other than travel advances [see 31 CFR 285.5 (e)(2)(vii)]
Department of Agriculture Department of Agriculture-continued	Department of Agriculture, Food and Nutrition Service benefit payments made under the following programs: * Food stamp program * Nutrition assistance program for Puerto Rico * Special supplemental nutrition program for women, infants, and children (WIC) * WIC farmers market nutrition program * National school lunch program * Summer food service program * Child and adult care food program * Special milk program for children * School breakfast program Payments made under the following Rural Development programs: * Multi-Family Rental Assistance program * Community Facilities direct loans and grants * Single Family Housing-Homeownership direct loans and grants * Single Family Housing-Technical Assistance grants * Multi-Family Housing direct loans and grants * Multi-Family Housing Preservation grants * Business and Industry direct loans * Intermediary Relending direct loans * Rural Business Opportunity grants * Rural Business Enterprise grants * Rural Economic Development direct loans * Water and Waste Disposal direct loans and grants
Department of Health and Human Services	Payments under the following: * Vaccine Injury Compensation Program (other than death benefits) * Tribal Law 93-638 Contracts/Compacts * National Institutes of Health Clinical Center patients * Ricky Ray Hemophilia Relief Fund Act of 1998 (Ricky Ray Fund) Payments to small, non-profit organizations and/or Indian Tribes/Tribal organizations serving areas for which no alternative organization is available to provide the grant-specific services under the following programs: * Head Start * Abandoned Infants * Native American * Transitional Living * Refugee Assistance-Voluntary Agency * Community Services Block Grant * Refugee and Entrant Assistance * Family Support Center and Gateway Demonstration

PAYMENTS EXEMPT BY ACTION OF THE SECRETARY OF THE TREASURY (31 U.S.C. § 3716(c)(3)(B))	
Payment Agency	**Type of Payment**
	* Runaway and Homeless Youth * Drug Education and Prevention for Homeless Youth * Youth Initiative and Youth Gangs * Older American Grants for Native Americans * Coverage Gap rebate payments for eligible Medicare Part D enrollees (temporary)
Department of Homeland Security - Federal Emergency Management Agency	Federal Emergency Management Agency payments under the following disaster relief and emergency assistance programs: * Assistance to Firefighters Grant Program * Cora Brown Fund (disaster aid) (CBF) * Community Disaster Loan (CDL) * Crisis Counseling Program (formerly known as Crisis Counseling Assistance and Training) * Disaster Case Management Program (DCMP) * Disaster Legal Services (DLS) * Fire Suppression Assistance/Fire Management Assistance Grant (FMAG) (formerly known as Fire Suppression Assistance) * Housing Assistance (formerly known as Disaster Housing; now under Individual and Households Program (IHP)) * Individual and Households Program (IHP), to include Housing Assistance (formerly known as Individual and Family Grant program) * Public Assistance (formerly known as Public Assistance to State and Local Governments) * Urban Search and Rescue (US&R)
Department of Housing and Urban Development	Payments under the following programs: * Annual Contributions for Operation of Low-Income Housing Projects * Contributions for Low-Income Housing Projects (Development) * Public Housing Modernization Program (Modernization) * Lease Adjustments * Section 8 Low-Income Housing Assistance (Rental Voucher Program) * Section 8 Counseling; Family Self Sufficiency (excluding payments for administrative costs) * Revitalization of Severely Distressed Public Housing (Hope VI) * Public and Assisted Housing Drug Elimination * Family Investment Centers * Indian Homeownership Program (Mutual Help Homeownership) grants * Hope 3 Program (HOPE for Homeownership of Single Family Homes) * Home Program (HOME Investment Partnerships) * Section 8 Payment * Rental Assistance Section 236 * Direct Loans for the Elderly or Handicapped Section 202 * Rental Supplements (Section 101) * Safe Neighborhood Grants * Drug Elimination Grants * Two Homeless Assistance Programs (Supportive Housing, Emergency Shelter Grants, Shelter Plus Care Program and Section 8 Moderate Rehabilitation Single Room Occupancy Program)

TREASURY OFFSET PROGRAM
Payments Exempt from Offset by Disbursing Officials
(Non-tax Debt Collection)

PAYMENTS EXEMPT BY ACTION OF THE SECRETARY OF THE TREASURY (31 U.S.C. § 3716(c)(3)(B))	
Payment Agency	**Type of Payment**
	* Home Equity Conversion Mortgage Program * Flexible Subsidy Program * Mark-to-Market Portfolio Reengineering Demonstration Program * Community Development Block Grants to municipal governments, counties and townships * Housing Opportunities for Persons with Acquired Immune Deficiency Syndrome (HOPWA) * Grants to Historically Black Colleges and Universities * Service Coordinator and Congregate Housing Services Programs
Department of the Interior	* Payments made to Indian tribes and tribal organizations under the provisions of the Indian Self-Determination and Education Assistance Act. * Payment made under Bureau of Indian Affairs Welfare Assistance Program * Payments made by the Office of the Special Trustee (OST) for American Indians to individual Indians from the Individual Indian Money (IIM) accounts * Payments made from the Natural Resource Damage Assessment and Restoration Fund to states and federally recognized Indian tribes and their entities
Department of Justice	* Payments to eligible claimants pursuant to the September 11th Victims Compensation Fund * Attorney fee payments made under prevailing party fee-shifting statutes to satisfy court judgments or settlements in actions certified as class actions pursuant to Federal Rule of Civil Procedure 23(b)(2) * Payments made by the U.S. Marshals Service (USMS) for the purpose of providing awards to confidential sources who have provided information or assistance directly related to violations of the criminal drug laws of the United States pursuant to 28 U.S.C. § 524(c)(1)(B) * Payments made by the Office of Justice Programs (OJP) through the International Victim Expense Reimbursement Program (ITVERP) for the purpose of providing funding for critical and ongoing medical treatment for victims of international terrorism * Payments associated with settlements of class actions certified under Federal Rule of Civil Procedure 23(b)(3) for attorney's fees and litigation costs for class counsel paid under prevailing party fee statutes and administrative costs of distributing settlements through the use of an administrator
Department of Transportation	* Payments made to Indian tribes and tribal organizations for the Indian Reservation Road program under the provisions of the Indian Self-Determination and Education Assistance Act (ISDEAA). *Tribal Transit Program payments made to Indian Tribes to provide public transportation on Indian reservations under the provisions of the Safe, Accountable, Flexible, Efficient, Transportation Equity Act: a Legacy of Users (SAFETEA-LU). * Federal Highway Administration and other Federal agencies authorized to make payments under the Uniform Relocation Assistance and Real Property Acquisition Policies Act of 1970 (Uniform Act) for displaced individuals and businesses.
Pension Benefit Guaranty Corporation	Pension Benefit Guaranty payments as follows: * Premium refunds to pension plans and plan sponsors * Financial assistance to multiemployer plans * Contractor bank payments to participants and beneficiaries

165

TREASURY OFFSET PROGRAM
Payments Exempt from Offset by Disbursing Officials
(Non-tax Debt Collection)

PAYMENTS EXEMPT BY ACTION OF THE SECRETARY OF THE TREASURY (31 U.S.C. § 3716(c)(3)(B))	
Payment Agency	**Type of Payment**
Public Defender Service for the District of Columbia	85% of disposable pay from salary payments paid to employees of the Public Defender Service for the District of Columbia
Department of the Treasury, Bureau of the Fiscal Service	State and Local Government Securities (SLGS) payments under this program: * Payments paid through this program are issued to state and local governments to pay off tax-exempt bond issues. * Payments are used to pay off investment funds used for investing in tax-exempt municipal bonds when a state or local municipality has sold them
Department of the Treasury, Office of District of Columbia Pensions	75% of payments made under the District of Columbia's Judges' Retirement Plan and the District of Columbia's Teachers' Retirement Plan and Police Officers' and Firefighters' Retirement Plan

Revised – May 2018

OMB Number: 1845-0146
Expiration Date: 12/31/2019

U.S. DEPARTMENT OF EDUCATION
APPLICATION FOR BORROWER DEFENSE
TO LOAN REPAYMENT

If your school misled you or engaged in other misconduct, you may be eligible for "borrower defense to repayment," which is the forgiveness of some or all of your federal student loan debt.

FORM INSTRUCTIONS: To apply, you must complete, sign, and submit this form to the U.S. Department of Education for review.

You may attach additional documents, such as transcripts, enrollment agreements, and promotional materials from your school. Once completed, please submit this form and any additional documents you believe will help us review your application by email to BorrowerDefense@ed.gov or mail to US Department of Education - Borrower Defense to Repayment, PO Box 1854, Monticello, KY 42633.

Fields marked with an asterisk (*) are required for your application to be considered complete.

SECTION I: BORROWER INFORMATION

Please provide contact information for the borrower:

*Name (First, Middle, Last)		*Date of Birth (mm/dd/yyyy)	*Social Security Number	
*Telephone Number	*Email Address			
*Street Address		*City	*State	*Zipcode

*Are you a PARENT who took out a federal loan on behalf of the student?

☐ Yes   ☐ No

*If yes, please enter the full name of the student (Last, First, Middle):

*If yes, please enter the student's Social Security Number:

SECTION II: SCHOOL INFORMATION

*School

Campus (including on-line campuses for distance education borrowers)

*Location (City, State)

* Enrollment Dates at this school:

*From (month/year):   *To (month/year):

☐ If you are still attending this school/campus, please indicate by checking the box.

☐ Check if the enrollment dates above are approximate, or if you are unsure of them.

If your attendance at the school listed above was not or has not been continuous (for example, from October 2015 to March 2016, then again from August 2016 to November 2016), please describe all dates that you attended.

*Program Name or Major (e.g. Nursing, Medical Assistant, Paralegal).

Credential/Degree Sought (e.g. Certificate, Diploma, Associates, Bachelors, Masters).

If you enrolled in multiple programs at the school listed above, please describe all programs that you were enrolled in.

*Current Status at school listed above

☐ Graduated   ☐ Transferred Out   ☐ Withdrew   ☐ Attending

SECTION III: OTHER LOAN REDUCTION OR TUITION RECOVERY REQUESTS

*Have you made any other requests to have your Federal loans forgiven (for example, under a closed school discharge or false certification discharge from the U.S. Department of Education)?

☐ Yes   ☐ No

*If yes, please describe these other request(s), including the amount of any loan forgiveness that you received, and attach any documentation about the requests, if available.

*Have you made any requests to anyone else to recover tuition amounts that you paid to your school (for example, a lawsuit against the school or a claim made to a tuition recovery program)?

☐ Yes   ☐ No

*If yes, please describe these other request(s), including the amount of the payment that you received (if any), and attach any documentation about the requests, if available.

SECTION IV. BASIS FOR BORROWER DEFENSE

Answer the questions for each section below that applies to you.

For each section below that applies to you, please provide a **detailed** description of why you believe you are entitled to borrower defense, including the following information:

1. How the school communicated with you, whether in a brochure, online, over the phone, by email, or in person

2. The name/title of people who you believe misled you (if known)

3. What the school told you or failed to tell you.

4. Why you believe you were misled.

Attach any related documents, such as transcripts, enrollment agreements, promotional materials from the school, emails with school officials or your school's manual, or course catalog.

Note: You only need to provide information for the sections below that apply to you, but you must complete at least one section. If you are a Parent PLUS borrower, the word "you" in the following sections also refers to the student.

If you need more space to complete any section, please attach additional pages to your application.

168

EMPLOYMENT PROSPECTS

Did the school mislead you *(or fail to tell you important information)* about promises of future employment, likelihood of finding a job, eligibility for certification or licensure in your field of study, how many students graduate, and/or earnings after graduation?

☐ Yes   ☐ No

If yes, you must provide <u>detailed</u> information about how the school misled you. Please also describe any financial harm to you as a result of the school's conduct.

*Did you choose to enroll in your school based in part on the issues you describe above?

☐ Yes   ☐ No

PROGRAM COST AND NATURE OF LOAN

Did the school mislead you *(or fail to tell you important information)* about how much your classes would cost, how you would pay for your education, the terms of loan repayment, and/or other issues about the cost of your education?

☐ Yes   ☐ No

If yes, you must provide <u>detailed</u> information about how the school misled you. Please also describe any financial harm to you as a result of the school's conduct.

*Did you choose to enroll in your school based in part on the issues you describe above?

☐ Yes   ☐ No

TRANSFERRING CREDITS

Did the school mislead you *(or fail to tell you important information)* about transferring your credits from this school to other schools?

☐ Yes   ☐ No

If yes, you must provide <u>detailed</u> information about how the school misled you. Please also describe any financial harm to you as a result of the school's conduct.

*Did you choose to enroll in your school based in part on the issues you describe above?

☐ Yes   ☐ No

CAREER SERVICES

Did the school mislead you *(or fail to tell you important information)* about the availability or quality of job placement, career services assistance, or the school's connections to employers within your field of study?

☐ Yes   ☐ No

If yes, you must provide <u>detailed</u> information about how the school misled you. Please also describe any financial harm to you as a result of the school's conduct.

*Did you choose to enroll in your school based in part on the issues you describe above?

☐ Yes   ☐ No

170

EDUCATIONAL SERVICES

Did the school mislead you *(or fail to tell you important information)* about educational services, such as the availability of externships, qualifications of teachers, instructional methods, or other types of educational services?

☐ Yes   ☐ No

If yes, you must provide detailed information about how the school misled you. Please also describe any financial harm to you as a result of the school's conduct.

*Did you choose to enroll in your school based in part on the issues you describe above?

☐ Yes   ☐ No

ADMISSIONS AND URGENCY TO ENROLL

Did the school mislead you *(or fail to tell you important information)* about the importance of enrolling immediately, the consequences of failure to enroll, how difficult it was to be admitted, or anything else about the admission process?

☐ Yes   ☐ No

If yes, you must provide detailed information about how the school misled you. Please also describe any financial harm to you as a result of the school's conduct.

*Did you choose to enroll in your school based in part on the issues you describe above?

☐ Yes   ☐ No

OTHER

Do you have any other reasons relating to your school that you believe qualify you for borrower defense, such as your school failing to perform its obligations under its contract with you, or that there is a judgment against your school in a Federal court, a State court, or in front of an administrative board or that you believe that you have a state law cause of action against the school?

☐ Yes ☐ No

Is there some other reason you feel your school misled you?

☐ Yes ☐ No

If yes, you must provide detailed information about how the school misled you. Please also describe any financial harm to you as a result of the school's conduct.

*Did you choose to enroll in your school based in part on the issues you describe above?

☐ Yes ☐ No

SECTION V: FORBEARANCE/STOPPED COLLECTIONS

If you are not currently in default on your federal student loans, you may request to have them placed into **forbearance** status while your application is under review. **Forbearance means that you do not have to make loan payments and your loans will not go into default.** Forbearance will continue until the borrower defense review process of your application is completed. Your servicer will notify you when your loans have been placed into forbearance status.

If your federal student loans are in **default**, you may request to have debt collection on your loan stopped ("**stopped collections status**"). **This means that the federal government or debt collection companies will stop attempting to collect on the loans, including by not withholding money from your wages or income tax refunds.** Stopped collections status will continue until the borrower defense review process of your application is completed.

Please see the "Common Questions and Answers Regarding Forbearance/Stopped Collections" section on the Borrower Defense website (https://studentaid.ed.gov/borrower-defense) if you have any questions regarding choosing to enter forbearance or stopped collections.

Note that interest will continue to accumulate on federal loans regardless of what status they are in, including subsidized loans. If your application for borrower defense is denied, or partially approved, the total amount you owe on those loans may be higher.

PLEASE NOTE: You do not have to place your loans in forbearance or stopped collections to apply for borrower defense relief.

For the most current information with regard to your rights and obligations regarding forbearance and stopped collections, please visit the Borrower Defense website at https://studentaid.gov/borrower-defense.

*Are you requesting forbearance/stopped collections?

☐ Yes, I want all of my federal loans currently in repayment to be placed in forbearance and for collections to stop on any loans in default while my borrower defense application is reviewed. During this time period, I understand that interest will continue to accrue.

☐ No, I do not want all of my federal loans currently in repayment to be placed in forbearance and for collections to stop on any loans in default while my borrower defense application is reviewed. During this time period, I understand that interest will continue to accrue and that I must continue to make loan payments.

If you do not select one of the options immediately above, your federal loans currently in repayment will automatically be placed into forbearance and collections will stop for any defaulted loans, and the Department will request forbearance for any commercially held Federal Family Education Loan (FFEL) program loans currently in repayment and for debt collection to stop for any defaulted, commercially held FFEL program loans that you have currently *(as applicable)*.

SECTION VI. CERTIFICATION

By signing this attestation I certify that:

All of the information I provided is true and complete to the best of my knowledge. Upon request, I agree to provide to the U.S. Department of Education information that is reasonably available to me that will verify the accuracy of my completed attestation.

I agree to provide, upon request, testimony, a sworn statement, or other documentation reasonably available to me that demonstrates to the satisfaction of the U.S. Department of Education or its designee that I meet the qualifications for borrower defense.

I certify that I received proceeds of a federal loan, in whole or in part, to attend the school/campus identified in Section II (above).

I understand that if my application is approved and some or all of my loans are forgiven, I am assigning to the U.S. Department of Education any legal claim I have against the school for those forgiven loans. By assigning my claims, I am effectively transferring my interests in any claim that I could make against the school relating to the forgiven loans (including the ability to file a lawsuit over those forgiven loans and any money ultimately recovered in compensation for those forgiven loans in court or other legal proceedings) to the U.S. Department of Education. I am not assigning any claims I may have against the school for any other form of relief --including injunctive relief or damages related to private loans, tuition paid out-of-pocket, unforgiven loans, or other losses.

I understand that the U.S. Department of Education has the authority to verify information reported on this application with other federal or state agencies or other entities. I authorize the U.S. Department of Education, along with its agents and contractors, to contact me regarding this request at the phone number above using automated dialing equipment or artificial or prerecorded voice or text messages.

I understand that any rights and obligations with regard to borrower defense to repayment are subject to the provisions currently in effect under Title 34 of the Code of Federal Regulations.

I understand that if I purposely provided false or misleading information on this application, I may be subject to the penalties specified in 18 U.S.C. § 1001, including fines. I understand that I may be asked to confirm the truthfulness of the statements in this application to the best of my knowledge under penalty of perjury.

*Signature	Date

Submit this form and any additional documents you believe will help us review your application by email to BorrowerDefense@ed.gov or by mail to: U.S. Department of Education - Borrower Defense to Repayment, PO Box 42633, Monticello, KY 42633.

Federal Direct Consolidation Loan Application and Promissory Note
William D. Ford Federal Direct Loan Program

OMB No. 1845-0053
Form Approved
Exp. Date 04/30/2016

WARNING: Any person who knowingly makes a false statement or misrepresentation on this form or any accompanying documentation is subject to penalties that may include fines, imprisonment, or both, under the U.S. Criminal Code and 20 U.S.C. 1097.

BEFORE YOU BEGIN

Read the Instructions for Completing the Federal Direct Consolidation Loan Application and Promissory Note ("Instructions").
NOTE: PAGES 1 THROUGH 5 MUST BE SUBMITTED FOR YOUR LOAN REQUEST TO BE PROCESSED.

BORROWER INFORMATION

1. Last Name: _____ First Name: _____ Middle Initial: _____

2. Former Name(s): _____

3. Social Security Number: __ __ __ - __ __ - __ __ __ __

4. Date of Birth: _____

5. Permanent Address (Street, City, State, Zip Code) (if P.O. box or general delivery, see Instructions):

6. Area Code/Telephone Number: _____

7. E-Mail Address (Optional): _____

8. Driver's License State and Number: _____

9. Employer's Name and Address (Street, City, State, Zip Code):

10. Work Area Code/Telephone Number: _____

REFERENCE INFORMATION

List 2 persons with different U.S. addresses who do not live with you and who have known you for at least 3 years.

11. Last Name: _____ First Name: _____ Middle Initial: _____

Permanent Address (Street, City, State, Zip Code):

E-Mail Address (optional): _____

Area Code/Telephone Number: _____

Relationship to You: _____

12. Last Name: _____ First Name: _____ Middle Initial: _____

Permanent Address (Street, City, State, Zip Code):

E-Mail Address (optional): _____

Area Code/Telephone Number: _____

Relationship to You: _____

Borrower's Name: _____   Social Security Number: __ __ __ - __ __ - __ __ __ __

LOANS YOU WANT TO CONSOLIDATE

Read the instructions before completing this section. List each federal education loan that you want to consolidate, including any Direct Loan Program loans that you want to include in your Direct Consolidation Loan. If you need more space to list loans, use the Additional Loan Listing Sheet included with this Note. List each loan separately.

We will send you a notice before we consolidate your loans. This notice will **(1)** provide you with information about the loans and payoff amounts that we have verified, and **(2)** tell you the deadline by which you must notify us if you want to cancel the Direct Consolidation Loan, or if you do not want to consolidate one or more of the loans listed in the notice. The notice will include information about loans that you listed in this section. If you have additional loans with a holder of a loan that you listed in this section, the notice may also include information about those additional loans. **See the Instructions for more information about the notice we will send.**

IN THIS SECTION, LIST ONLY LOANS THAT YOU WANT TO CONSOLIDATE

13. Loan Code (see Instructions)	14. Loan Holder/Servicer Name, Address, and Area Code/Telephone Number (see Instructions)	15. Loan Account Number	16. Estimated Payoff Amount

17. Grace Period End Date. If any of the loans you want to consolidate are in a grace period, you can have the processing of your Direct Consolidation Loan delayed until the end of your grace period by entering your expected grace period end date in the space provided.

If you leave this item blank, we will begin processing your Direct Consolidation Loan as soon as we receive this Note and any other required documents. Any loans listed in the **Loans You Want to Consolidate** section that are in a grace period will enter repayment immediately upon consolidation. You will then lose the remaining portion of the grace period on those loans.

Expected Grace Period End Date (month/year): _____

Borrower's Name: _____   Social Security Number: __ __ __ - __ __ - __ __ __ __

LOANS YOU DO NOT WANT TO CONSOLIDATE

Read the instructions before completing this section. List all education loans that you are not consolidating, but want us to consider when we calculate the maximum repayment period for your Direct Consolidation Loan (see Item 11 of the **Borrower's Rights and Responsibilities Statement** that accompanies this Note). Remember to include any Direct Loan Program loans that you do not want to consolidate. If you need more space to list loans, use the Additional Loan Listing Sheet included with this Note. List each loan separately.

We will send you a notice before we consolidate your loans. This notice will **(1)** provide you with information about the loans and payoff amounts that we have verified, and **(2)** tell you the deadline by which you must notify us if you want to cancel the Direct Consolidation Loan, or if you do not want to consolidate one or more of the loans listed in the notice. The notice may also include information about any loans you listed in this section, but these loans listed will **not** be consolidated. **See the Instructions for more information about the notice we will send.**

IN THIS SECTION, LIST ONLY LOANS THAT YOU DO NOT WANT TO CONSOLIDATE

18. Loan Code (see Instructions)	19. Loan Holder/Servicer Name, Address, and Area Code/Telephone Number (see Instructions)	20. Loan Account Number	21. Current Balance

REPAYMENT PLAN SELECTION

To understand your repayment plan options, carefully read the repayment plan information in Item 11 of the **Borrower's Rights and Responsibilities Statement** that accompanies this Note and in any supplemental materials you receive with this Note. Then select a repayment plan for your Direct Consolidation Loan:

- To select the Standard Repayment Plan, the Graduated Repayment Plan, or the Extended Repayment Plan, complete the **Repayment Plan Selection** form that accompanies this Note.
- To select the Income-Based Repayment Plan (IBR Plan), the Pay As You Earn Repayment Plan (Pay As You Earn Plan), or the Income-Contingent Repayment Plan (ICR Plan), visit StudentLoans.gov to complete the application online or complete the **Income-Driven Repayment Plan Request** form that accompanies this Note.

NOTE: You **must** select the IBR Plan, the Pay As You Earn Plan, or the ICR Plan for repayment of your Direct Consolidation Loan if:

1. You want to consolidate a defaulted loan and you have not made a satisfactory repayment arrangement with your current loan holder(s); or

2. You are consolidating a delinquent Federal Consolidation Loan that the lender has submitted to the guaranty agency for default aversion, or you are consolidating a defaulted Federal Consolidation Loan, and you are not consolidating any additional eligible loans.

BORROWER UNDERSTANDINGS, CERTIFICATIONS, AND AUTHORIZATIONS

22. I understand that:

A. Applying for a Direct Consolidation Loan does not obligate me to agree to take the loan. The U.S. Department of Education (ED) will provide me with:

- The deadline by which I must notify ED if I want to cancel the Direct Consolidation Loan, or if I do not want to consolidate any of the loans that ED has verified; and
- A notice containing information about the loans and payoff amounts that ED has verified with the holders of my loans or through ED's National Student Loan Data System (NSLDS) before the actual payoffs occur.

The notice that ED sends will include information about the loans I listed in the **Loans You Want to Consolidate** section of this Note. If I have additional loans that are with a holder of a loan listed in the **Loans You Want to Consolidate** section, but I did not list those loans in that section, the notice may also include information about those additional loans. **I must inform ED by the deadline specified in the notice if I do not want all of the loans listed in the notice to be consolidated.**

The notice that ED sends may also include information about loans I listed in the **Loans You Do Not Want to Consolidate** section of this Note, but these loans will **not** be consolidated.

176

BORROWER UNDERSTANDINGS, CERTIFICATIONS, AND AUTHORIZATIONS (CONTINUED)

B. If ED accepts this application for a Direct Consolidation Loan, I understand that ED will send funds to the holders of the loans that I want to consolidate to pay off those loans. The amount of my Direct Consolidation Loan will be the sum of the balances of my outstanding eligible loans that I have chosen to consolidate. The payoff amount may be greater than or less than the estimated total balance I have indicated in the **Loans You Want to Consolidate** section.

The outstanding balance on each loan to be consolidated includes unpaid principal, unpaid accrued interest and late charges as defined by federal regulations and as certified by the loan holder. Collection costs may also be included. For a Direct Loan Program or Federal Family Education Loan (FFEL) Program loan that is in default, the amount of any collection costs that may be included in the payoff balances of the loans is limited to a maximum of 18.5% of the outstanding principal and interest. For any other defaulted federal education loans, all collection costs that are owed may be included in the payoff balances of the loans.

C. If the amount ED sends to my loan holders is more than the amount needed to pay off the balances of the selected loans, the holders will refund the excess amount to ED and this amount will be applied against the outstanding balance of my Direct Consolidation Loan. If the amount that ED sends to my holders is less than the amount needed to pay off the balances of the loans selected for consolidation, ED will include the remaining amount in my Direct Consolidation Loan.

D. If I am consolidating loans made under the FFEL, Direct Loan, or Federal Perkins Loan (Perkins Loan) programs, the outstanding balance of my Direct Consolidation Loan counts against the applicable aggregate loan limits for each type of loan. Under the Act ("the Act" is defined under "Governing Law" in the **Note Terms and Conditions** section of this Note), the percentage of the original amount of my Direct Consolidation Loan that is attributable to each loan type is counted against the loan limit for that type of loan.

E. I must agree to repay my Direct Consolidation Loan under the IBR Plan, the Pay As You Earn Plan, or the ICR Plan if:

- I am consolidating a defaulted loan and I have not made a satisfactory repayment arrangement with the current holder of the defaulted loan, or

- I am consolidating a delinquent Federal Consolidation Loan (a consolidation loan made under the FFEL Program) that the lender has submitted to the guaranty agency for default aversion or a defaulted Federal Consolidation Loan, and I am not including another eligible loan in the consolidation.

F. I may not consolidate an existing Direct Consolidation Loan unless I include at least one additional eligible loan in the consolidation. I may consolidate an existing Federal Consolidation Loan without including an additional eligible loan in the consolidation if I am:

- Consolidating a delinquent Federal Consolidation Loan that the lender has submitted to the guaranty agency for default aversion, or consolidating a defaulted Federal Consolidation Loan, and I agree to repay my new Direct Consolidation Loan under the IBR Plan, the Pay As You Earn Plan, or the ICR Plan;

- Consolidating a Federal Consolidation Loan to use the Public Service Loan Forgiveness Program; or

- Consolidating a Federal Consolidation Loan to use the no accrual of interest benefit for active duty service members.

G. If I consolidate my loans, I may no longer be eligible for certain deferments, subsidized deferment periods, certain types of loan discharges or loan forgiveness, reduced interest rates, or repayment incentive programs that were available on the loans I am consolidating.

H. If I am consolidating a Perkins Loan:

- I will no longer be eligible for interest-free periods while I am enrolled in school at least half time, in the grace period on my loan, and during deferment periods; and

- I will no longer be eligible for full or partial loan cancellation under the Perkins Loan Program based on years of service in one of the following occupations: teacher in a low-income elementary or secondary school; staff member in an eligible preschool program; special education teacher; member of the Armed Forces who qualifies for special pay; Peace Corps volunteer or volunteer under the Domestic Volunteer Service Act of 1973; law enforcement or corrections officer; attorney in an eligible defender organization; teacher of mathematics, science, foreign languages, bilingual education or any other high-need field; nurse or medical technician providing health care services; employee of a public or private nonprofit child or family service agency that services high-risk children from low-income families and their families; fire fighter; faculty member at a Tribal College or University; librarian; or speech language pathologist.

I. Any payments I made on the loans I am consolidating before the date of consolidation will not count toward:

- The number of years of qualifying repayment required for loan forgiveness under the IBR Plan, the Pay As You Earn Plan, or the ICR Plan (see Item 11 of the **Borrower's Rights and Responsibilities Statement**), or

- The 120 qualifying payments required for Public Service Loan Forgiveness (see Item 18 of the **Borrower's Rights and Responsibilities Statement**).

J. If I am consolidating a Direct PLUS Loan or a Federal PLUS Loan that I obtained to help pay for my child's undergraduate education, I will not be eligible to repay my Direct Consolidation Loan under the IBR Plan or the Pay As You Earn Plan. However, I may repay my Direct Consolidation Loan under the ICR Plan.

K. If I am consolidating a Direct Loan Program loan first disbursed before July 1, 2012 on which I received an up-front interest rebate, and I have not yet made the first 12 required on-time payments on that loan at the time the loan is consolidated, I will lose the rebate. This means that the rebate amount will be added back to the principal balance of the loan before it is consolidated.

L. ED will give me the opportunity to pay the interest that accrues on the unsubsidized portion of my Direct Consolidation Loan during deferment periods (including in-school deferment periods) and on the entire portion of my Direct Consolidation Loan during forbearance periods. If I do not pay the interest that accrues during these periods, ED may add the unpaid interest that accrues to the principal balance of my loan (this is called "capitalization") at the end of the deferment or forbearance period. Capitalization will increase the principal balance on my loan and the total amount of interest I must pay.

BORROWER UNDERSTANDINGS, CERTIFICATIONS, AND AUTHORIZATIONS (CONTINUED)

M. ED has the authority to verify information reported on this Note with other federal agencies.

23. Under penalty of perjury, I certify that:

A. The information that I have provided on this Note is true, complete, and correct to the best of my knowledge and belief and is made in good faith.

B. All of the loans I have selected for consolidation have been used to finance my education or the education of one or more of my children.

C. All of the loans I have selected for consolidation are in a grace period or in repayment ("in repayment" includes loans in deferment or forbearance).

D. If I owe an overpayment on a Federal Perkins Loan, Federal Pell Grant, Federal Supplemental Educational Opportunity Grant, Academic Competitiveness Grant (ACG), National Science and Mathematics Access to Retain Talent (SMART) Grant, or Leveraging Educational Assistance Partnership Grant, I have made satisfactory arrangements to repay the amount owed.

E. If I am in default on any loan I am consolidating, I have either made a satisfactory repayment arrangement with the holder of that defaulted loan, or I will repay my Direct Consolidation Loan under the IBR Plan, the Pay As You Earn Plan, or the ICR Plan, except that I **must** repay my Direct Consolidation Loan under the IBR Plan, the Pay As You Earn Plan, or the ICR Plan under the conditions described above in Item 22.E.

F. If I have been convicted of, or if I have pled *nolo contendere* (no contest) or guilty to, a crime involving fraud in obtaining funds under Title IV of the Higher Education Act of 1965, as amended (HEA), I have fully repaid the funds to ED or to the loan holder in the case of a Title IV federal student loan.

24. I make the following authorizations:

A. I authorize ED to contact the holders of the loans I have selected for consolidation to determine the eligibility for consolidation and the payoff amounts of:

- The loans listed in the **Loans You Want to Consolidate** section of this Note, and

- Any of my other federal education loans that are held by a holder of a loan listed in the **Loans You Want to Consolidate** section.

I further authorize the release of any information required to consolidate my education loans, in accordance with the Act, to ED or its agents and contractors.

B. I authorize ED to issue the proceeds of my Direct Consolidation Loan to the holders of the selected loans to pay off those loans.

C. I authorize ED to investigate my credit record and report information about my loan status to persons and organizations permitted by law to receive that information.

D. I authorize my schools, ED, and their agents and contractors to release information about my Direct Consolidation Loan to the references on the loan and to my immediate family members, unless I submit written directions otherwise.

E. I authorize my schools, ED, and their agents and contractors to share information about my loan with each other.

F. I authorize my schools, ED, and their agents and contractors to contact me regarding my loan request or my loan, including repayment of my loan, at the number that I provide on this Note or any future number that I provide for my cellular telephone or other wireless device using automated dialing equipment or artificial or prerecorded voice or text messages.

PROMISE TO PAY

25. I promise to pay ED all sums disbursed under the terms of this Note to pay off my prior loan obligations, plus interest and other charges and fees that may become due as provided in this Note.

26. If I do not make a payment on my Direct Consolidation Loan when it is due, I will also pay reasonable collection costs, including but not limited to attorney fees, court costs, and other fees.

27. My signature on this Note serves as my authorization to pay off the balances of the loans I have selected for consolidation as provided by the holders of the loans.

28. I will not sign this Note before reading the entire Note, even if I am told not to read it, or told that I am not required to read it. I am entitled to an exact copy of this Note and the **Borrower's Rights and Responsibilities Statement** .

29. My signature certifies that I have read, understand, and agree to the terms and conditions of this Note, including the **Borrower Understandings, Certifications, and Authorizations** section, and the **Borrower's Rights and Responsibilities Statement.**

I UNDERSTAND THAT THIS IS A LOAN THAT I MUST REPAY.

30. Borrower's Signature:

_____

Today's Date (mm-dd-yyyy) _____

THIS PAGE IS INTENTIONALLY BLANK

NOTE TERMS AND CONDITIONS

GOVERNING LAW

The terms of this Federal Direct Consolidation Loan Application and Promissory Note (Note) will be interpreted in accordance with the Higher Education Act of 1965, as amended (20 U.S.C. 1070 et seq.), the U.S. Department of Education's (ED's) regulations, any amendments to the HEA and the regulations in accordance with the effective date of those amendments, and other applicable federal laws and regulations (collectively referred to as the "Act").

Under applicable state law, except as preempted by federal law, you may have certain borrower rights, remedies, and defenses in addition to those stated in this Note and in the **Borrower's Rights and Responsibilities Statement** .

DISCLOSURE OF LOAN TERMS

This Note applies to a Federal Direct Consolidation Loan (Direct Consolidation Loan). Under this Note, the principal amount that you owe and are required to repay will be equal to all sums disbursed to pay off your prior loan obligations, plus any unpaid interest that is capitalized and added to the principal balance.

Although you will have a single Direct Consolidation Loan, your loan may have up to two separate loan identification numbers depending on the loans you consolidate. These loan identification numbers will represent prior subsidized loans and prior unsubsidized loans. Each applicable loan identification number is represented by this Note.

When the loans you are consolidating are paid off, a disclosure statement will be provided to you. The disclosure will identify the amount of your Direct Consolidation Loan, the loan identification number(s), and additional terms of the loan, such as the interest rate and repayment schedule. If you have questions about the information disclosed, you may contact your servicer. The **Borrower's Rights and Responsibilities Statement** accompanying this Note also contains important additional information. The **Borrower's Rights and Responsibilities Statement** and any disclosure you receive in connection with the loan made under this Note are hereby incorporated into this Note.

ED may use a servicer to handle billing and other communications related to your loan.

INTEREST

Unless ED notifies you in writing that a different rate will apply, the interest rate on your Direct Consolidation Loan is a fixed rate that is calculated in accordance with a formula specified in the Act. The interest rate for a Direct Consolidation Loan is based on the weighted average of the interest rates on the loans being consolidated, rounded to the nearest higher one-eighth of one percent. There is no cap on the interest rate that is determined under this formula. This is a fixed interest rate, which means that the rate will remain the same throughout the life of the loan.

Except as provided under the Act, you must pay the interest that accrues on your Direct Consolidation Loan during all periods, from the date of disbursement until the loan is paid in full or discharged. You are not required to pay the interest that accrues during deferment periods on the portion of your Direct Consolidation Loan that repaid subsidized loans, except as explained under the heading "Responsibility for Paying All Interest on All or Part of the Subsidized Portion of a Direct Consolidation Loan (for First-Time Borrowers on or after July 1, 2013)."

You will be given the opportunity to pay the interest that accrues during deferment, forbearance, or other periods as provided under the Act. If you do not pay this interest, ED may capitalize the interest (add it to the principal balance of your loan) at the end of the deferment, forbearance, or other period.

RESPONSIBILITY FOR PAYING ALL INTEREST ON ALL OR PART OF THE SUBSIDIZED PORTION OF A DIRECT CONSOLIDATION LOAN (FOR FIRST-TIME BORROWERS ON OR AFTER JULY 1, 2013)

If you were a **first-time borrower on or after July 1, 2013** when you received a Direct Subsidized Loan and you are now consolidating that loan, you may be responsible for paying the interest that accrues during all periods on the portion of your Direct Consolidation Loan that repaid the Direct Subsidized Loan. See Item 9 of the **Borrower's Rights and Responsibilities Statement** that accompanies this Note for more information.

LATE CHARGES AND COLLECTION COSTS

ED may collect from you:

- A late charge of not more than six cents for each dollar of each late payment if you fail to make any part of a required installment payment within 30 days after it becomes due, and

- Any other charges and fees that are permitted by the Act related to the collection of your Direct Consolidation Loan.

If you default on your loan, you must pay reasonable collection costs, plus court costs and attorney fees.

REPAYMENT

You must repay the full amount of the Direct Consolidation Loan made under this Note, plus accrued interest. You will repay your loan in monthly installments during a repayment period that begins on the date of the first disbursement of the loan, unless the loan is in a deferment or forbearance period. Generally, payments that you make or that someone else makes on your behalf will be applied first to late charges and collection costs that are due, then to interest that has not been paid, and finally to the principal amount of the loan. However, any payments made under the Income-Based Repayment Plan or the Pay As You Earn Repayment Plan will be applied first to interest that is due, then to fees that are due, and then to the principal amount.

ED will provide you with a choice of repayment plans. The **Borrower's Rights and Responsibilities Statement** includes information on these repayment plans. You must select a repayment plan. If you do not select a repayment plan, ED will choose a plan for you in accordance with the Act.

ED will provide you with a repayment schedule that identifies your payment amounts and due dates. Your first payment will be due within 60 days of the first disbursement of your Direct Consolidation Loan unless the loan is in a deferment or forbearance period. If you intend to repay your loan but are unable to make your scheduled loan payments, ED may grant you a forbearance that allows you to temporarily stop making payments, or to temporarily make a smaller payment amount, which extends the time for making payments.

ED may adjust payment dates on your Direct Consolidation Loan or may grant you a forbearance to eliminate a delinquency that remains even though you are making scheduled installment payments.

You may prepay all or any part of the unpaid balance on your loan at any time without penalty. After you have repaid your Direct Consolidation Loan in full, ED will send you a notice telling you that you have paid off your loan.

ACCELERATION AND DEFAULT

At ED's option, the entire unpaid balance of your Direct Consolidation Loan will become immediately due and payable (this is called "acceleration") if either of the following events occurs:

1. You make a false representation that results in your receiving a loan for which you are not eligible; or

2. You default on the loan.

The following events will constitute a default on your loan:

1. You do not pay the entire unpaid balance of the loan after ED has exercised its option under item 1 above;

2. You do not make installment payments when due and your failure to make payments has continued for at least 270 days; or

3. You do not comply with other terms of the loan, and ED reasonably concludes that you no longer intend to honor your repayment obligation.

If you default, ED may capitalize all outstanding interest. This will increase the principal balance of your loan, and the full amount of the loan, including the new principal balance and collection costs, will become immediately due and payable.

If you default, the default will be reported to nationwide consumer reporting agencies (credit bureaus) and will significantly and adversely affect your credit history. A default will have additional adverse consequences as explained in the **Borrower's Rights and Responsibilities Statement**. Following default, you may be required to repay the loan (potentially including amounts in excess of the principal and interest) under the Income-Based Repayment Plan or the Income-Contingent Repayment Plan in accordance with the Act.

LEGAL NOTICES

Any notice required to be given to you will be effective if sent by first class mail to the most recent address that ED has for you, by electronic means to an address you have provided, or by any other method of notification that is permitted or required by applicable statute or regulation.

You must immediately notify ED of a change in your contact information or status as specified in the **Borrower's Rights and Responsibilities Statement** under "Information you must report to us."

If ED does not enforce or insist on compliance with any term of this Note, this does not waive any right of ED. No provision of this Note may be modified or waived except in writing by ED. If any provision of this Note is determined to be unenforceable, the remaining provisions will remain in force.

Information about your loan will be submitted to the National Student Loan Data System (NSLDS). Information in NSLDS is accessible to schools, lenders, and guarantors for specific purposes as authorized by ED.

IMPORTANT NOTICES

Gramm-Leach-Bliley Act Notice

In 1999, Congress enacted the Gramm-Leach-Bliley Act (Public Law 106-102). This Act requires that lenders provide certain information to their customers regarding the collection and use of nonpublic personal information.

We disclose nonpublic personal information to third parties only as necessary to process and service your loan and as permitted by the Privacy Act of 1974. See the Privacy Act Notice below. We do not sell or otherwise make available any information about you to any third parties for marketing purposes.

We protect the security and confidentiality of nonpublic personal information by implementing the following policies and practices. All physical access to the sites where nonpublic personal information is maintained is controlled and monitored by security personnel. Our computer systems offer a high degree of resistance to tampering and circumvention. These systems limit data access to our staff and contract staff on a "need-to-know" basis, and control individual users' ability to access and alter records within the systems. All users of these systems are given a unique user ID with personal identifiers. All interactions by individual users with the systems are recorded.

Privacy Act Notice

The Privacy Act of 1974 (5 U.S.C. 552a) requires that the following notice be provided to you:

The authority for collecting the requested information from and about you is §451 et seq. of the Higher Education Act (HEA) of 1965, as amended (20 U.S.C. 1087a et seq.) and the authorities for collecting and using your Social Security Number (SSN) are §484(a)(4) of the HEA (20 U.S.C. 1091(a)(4)) and 31 U.S.C. 7701(b). Participating in the William D. Ford Federal Direct Loan (Direct Loan) Program and giving us your SSN are voluntary, but you must provide the requested information, including your SSN, to participate.

The principal purposes for collecting the information on this form, including your SSN, are to verify your identity, to determine your eligibility to receive a loan or a benefit on a loan (such as a deferment, forbearance, discharge, or forgiveness) under the Direct Loan Program, to permit the servicing of your loan(s), and, if it becomes necessary, to locate you and to collect and report on your loan(s) if your loan(s) become delinquent or in default. We also use your SSN as an account identifier and to permit you to access your account information electronically.

The information in your file may be disclosed, on a case-by-case basis or under a computer matching program, to third parties as authorized under routine uses in the appropriate systems of records notices. The routine uses of this information include, but are not limited to, its disclosure to federal, state, or local agencies, to private parties such as relatives, present and former employers, business and personal associates, to consumer reporting agencies, to financial and educational institutions, and to guaranty agencies in order to verify your identity, to determine your eligibility to receive a loan or a benefit on a loan, to permit the servicing or collection of your loan(s), to enforce the terms of the loan(s), to investigate possible fraud and to verify compliance with federal student financial aid program regulations, or to locate you if you become delinquent in your loan payments or if you default. To provide default rate calculations, disclosures may be made to guaranty agencies, to financial and educational institutions, or to state agencies. To provide financial aid history information, disclosures may be made to educational institutions. To assist program administrators with tracking refunds and cancellations, disclosures may be made to guaranty agencies, to financial and educational institutions, or to federal or state agencies. To provide a standardized method for educational institutions to efficiently submit student enrollment status, disclosures may be made to guaranty agencies or to financial and educational institutions. To counsel

you in repayment efforts, disclosures may be made to guaranty agencies, to financial and educational institutions, or to federal, state, or local agencies. In the event of litigation, we may send records to the Department of Justice, a court, adjudicative body, counsel, party, or witness if the disclosure is relevant and necessary to the litigation. If this information, either alone or with other information, indicates a potential violation of law, we may send it to the appropriate authority for action. We may send information to members of Congress if you ask them to help you with federal student aid questions. In circumstances involving employment complaints, grievances, or disciplinary actions, we may disclose relevant records to adjudicate or investigate the issues. If provided for by a collective bargaining agreement, we may disclose records to a labor organization recognized under 5 U.S.C. Chapter 71. Disclosures may be made to our contractors for the purpose of performing any programmatic function that requires disclosure of records. Before making any such disclosure, we will require the contractor to maintain Privacy Act safeguards. Disclosures may also be made to qualified researchers under Privacy Act safeguards.

Financial Privacy Act Notice

Under the Right to Financial Privacy Act of 1978 (12 U.S.C. 3401-3421), ED will have access to financial records in your student loan file maintained in compliance with the administration of the Direct Loan Program.

Paperwork Reduction Notice

According to the Paperwork Reduction Act of 1995, no persons are required to respond to a collection of information unless the collection displays a valid OMB control number. The valid OMB control number for this information collection is 1845-0053. Public reporting burden for this collection of information is estimated to average 30 minutes (0.5 hours) per response, including time for reviewing instructions, searching existing data sources, gathering and maintaining the data needed, and completing and reviewing the collection of information. The obligation to respond to this collection is required to obtain a benefit in accordance with 34 CFR 685.201(c)(1).

If you have comments or concerns regarding the status of your individual submission of this form, contact:

Important Notice:

*This Borrower's Rights and Responsibilities Statement provides additional information about the terms and conditions of the loan you will receive under the accompanying Federal Direct Consolidation Loan (Direct Consolidation Loan) Application and Promissory Note (Note). **Please keep a copy of the Note and this Borrower's Rights and Responsibilities Statement for your records.** You may request another copy of this Borrower's Rights and Responsibilities Statement at any time by contacting your servicer.*

Throughout this Borrower's Rights and Responsibilities Statement, the words "we," "us," and "our" refer to the U.S. Department of Education.

1. THE WILLIAM D. FORD FEDERAL DIRECT LOAN PROGRAM

The William D. Ford Federal Direct Loan (Direct Loan) Program includes the following types of loans, known collectively as "Direct Loans":

- Federal Direct Stafford/Ford Loans (Direct Subsidized Loans)
- Federal Direct Unsubsidized Stafford/Ford Loans (Direct Unsubsidized Loans)
- Federal Direct PLUS Loans (Direct PLUS Loans)
- Federal Direct Consolidation Loans (Direct Consolidation Loans)

The Direct Loan Program is authorized by Title IV, Part D, of the Higher Education Act of 1965, as amended (HEA), 20 U.S.C. 1070 et seq.

Direct Loans are made by the U.S. Department of Education. We contract with servicers to process Direct Loan payments, deferment and forbearance requests, and other transactions, and to answer questions about Direct Loans. We will provide you with the address and telephone number of the servicer for your loan.

2. LAWS THAT APPLY TO THIS NOTE

The terms and conditions of loans made under this Note are determined by the HEA and other applicable federal laws and regulations. These laws and regulations are referred to as "the Act" throughout this Borrower's Rights and Responsibilities Statement. Under applicable state law, except as preempted by federal law, you may have certain borrower rights, remedies, and defenses in addition to those stated in the Note and this Borrower's Rights and Responsibilities Statement.

NOTE: Any amendment to the Act that affects the terms of this Note will be applied to your loan in accordance with the effective date of the amendment.

3. DIRECT CONSOLIDATION LOAN IDENTIFICATION NUMBERS

Depending on the type(s) of federal education loan(s) that you choose to consolidate, your Direct Consolidation Loan may have up to two individual loan identification numbers. However, you will have only one Direct Consolidation Loan and will receive only one bill.

3a. The subsidized portion of your Direct Consolidation Loan ("Direct Subsidized Consolidation Loan") will have one loan identification number representing the amount of the following types of loans that you consolidate:

- Subsidized Federal Stafford Loans
- Direct Subsidized Loans
- Subsidized Federal Consolidation Loans
- Direct Subsidized Consolidation Loans
- Federal Insured Student Loans (FISL)
- Guaranteed Student Loans (GSL)

3b. The unsubsidized portion of your Direct Consolidation Loan ("Direct Unsubsidized Consolidation Loan") will have one identification number representing the amount of the following types of loans that you consolidate:

- Unsubsidized and Nonsubsidized Federal Stafford Loans
- Direct Unsubsidized Loans
- Unsubsidized Federal Consolidation Loans
- Direct Unsubsidized Consolidation Loans
- Federal PLUS Loans (for parents or for graduate and professional students)
- Direct PLUS Loans (for parents or for graduate and professional students)
- Direct PLUS Consolidation Loans
- Federal Perkins Loans
- National Direct Student Loans (NDSL)
- National Defense Student Loans (NDSL)
- Federal Supplemental Loans for Students (SLS)
- Parent Loans for Undergraduate Students (PLUS)
- Auxiliary Loans to Assist Students (ALAS)
- Health Professions Student Loans (HPSL)
- Health Education Assistance Loans (HEAL)
- Nursing Student Loans (NSL)
- Loans for Disadvantaged Students (LDS)

4. ADDING ELIGIBLE LOANS TO YOUR DIRECT CONSOLIDATION LOAN

You may add eligible loans to your Direct Consolidation Loan by submitting a request to us within 180 days of the date your Direct Consolidation Loan is made. (Your Direct Consolidation Loan is "made" on the date we pay off the first loan that you are consolidating.) After we pay off any loans that you add during the 180-day period, we will notify you of the new total amount of your Direct Consolidation Loan and of any adjustments that must be made to your monthly payment amount and/or interest rate.

If you want to consolidate any additional eligible loan(s) after the 180-day period, you must apply for a new Direct Consolidation Loan.

5. LOANS THAT MAY BE CONSOLIDATED

General

Only the federal education loans listed in Items 3a.and 3b. of this Borrower's Rights and Responsibilities Statement may be consolidated into a Direct Consolidation Loan. You may only consolidate loans that are in a grace period or in repayment (including loans in deferment or forbearance). At least one of the loans that you consolidate must be a Direct Loan Program loan or a Federal Family Education Loan (FFEL) Program loan.

Defaulted loans

You may consolidate a loan that is in default if:

- You first make satisfactory repayment arrangements with the holder of the defaulted loan, or
- You agree to repay your Direct Consolidation Loan under the IBR Plan, the Pay As You Earn Plan, or the ICR Plan (see Item 11).

Existing consolidation loans

If you want to consolidate an existing Direct Consolidation Loan, you must include an additional eligible loan in the consolidation. However, you may consolidate an existing Federal Consolidation Loan into a new Direct Consolidation Loan without including an additional loan if you are:

- Consolidating a delinquent Federal Consolidation Loan that the lender has submitted to the guaranty agency for default aversion, or consolidating a defaulted Federal Consolidation Loan, and you agree to repay your new Direct Consolidation Loan under the IBR Plan, the Pay As You Earn Plan, or the ICR Plan;

- Consolidating a Federal Consolidation Loan to use the Public Service Loan Forgiveness program described in Item 18 of this Borrower's Rights and Responsibilities Statement; or

- Consolidating a Federal Consolidation Loan to use the no accrual of interest benefit for active duty service members described in Item 8.

You may not consolidate an existing joint consolidation loan. A joint consolidation loan is a Direct Consolidation Loan or Federal Consolidation that was made jointly to you and your spouse.

6. INFORMATION YOU MUST REPORT TO US

Until your loan is repaid, you must notify your servicer if you:

- Change your address or telephone number;
- Change your name (for example, maiden name to married name);
- Change your employer or your employer's address or telephone number changes; or
- Have any other change in status that would affect your loan (for example, if you receive a deferment while you are unemployed, but you find a job and therefore no longer meet the eligibility requirements for the deferment).

7. INTEREST RATE

The interest rate on your Direct Consolidation Loan will be the weighted average of the interest rates on the loans you are consolidating, rounded to the nearest higher one-eighth of one percent. There is no cap on the interest rate that is determined under this formula. We will send you a notice that tells you the interest rate on your loan.

The interest rate on a Direct Consolidation Loan is a fixed rate. This means that the interest rate will remain the same throughout the life of your loan.

If you qualify under the Servicemembers Civil Relief Act, the interest rate on your loans obtained prior to military service may be limited to 6% during your military service. Contact your servicer for information about how to request this benefit.

8. PAYMENT OF INTEREST

General

In general, interest accrues on a Direct Consolidation Loan from the date the loan is made until it is paid in full or discharged. You are responsible for paying the interest that accrues as explained below.

Payment of interest on a Direct Subsidized Consolidation Loan

Except as explained in Item 9 of this Borrower's Rights and Responsibilities Statement, you are not required to pay the interest that accrues on a Direct Subsidized Consolidation Loan (see Item 3a. of this Borrower's Rights and Responsibilities Statement) during deferment periods, and during certain periods of repayment under the IBR Plan and the Pay As You Earn Plan. Except as explained below under *No accrual of interest benefit for active duty service members*, you must pay the interest that accrues on a Direct Subsidized Consolidation Loan during all other periods.

If you were a first-time borrower on or after July 1, 2013 when you received a Direct Subsidized Loan that you are now consolidating, you may be responsible for paying the interest that accrues during all periods on the

portion of your Direct Consolidation Loan that repaid the Direct Subsidized Loan, as explained in Item 9 of this Borrower's Rights and Responsibilities Statement.

Payment of interest on a Direct Unsubsidized Consolidation Loan

Except as explained below for certain borrowers who are active duty service members, you must pay the interest that accrues on a Direct Unsubsidized Consolidation Loan (see Item 3b. of this Borrower's Rights and Responsibilities Statement) during all periods.

No accrual of interest benefit for active duty service members

Under the no accrual of interest benefit for active duty service members, you are not required to pay the interest that accrues during periods of qualifying active duty military service (for up to 60 months) on the portion of a Direct Consolidation Loan that repaid a Direct Loan Program or FFEL Program loan first disbursed on or after October 1, 2008.

Interest capitalization

If you do not pay the interest as it accrues on either a Direct Subsidized Consolidation Loan or a Direct Unsubsidized Consolidation Loan (during periods when you are responsible for paying the interest), we will add the accrued interest to the unpaid principal balance of your loan at the end of the deferment or forbearance period. This is called "capitalization." Capitalization increases the unpaid principal balance of your loan, and interest then accrues on the increased principal balance.

The chart that follows shows the difference in the total amount you would repay on a $15,000 Direct Unsubsidized Consolidation Loan if you pay the interest as it accrues during a 12-month deferment or forbearance period, compared to the amount you would repay if you do not pay the interest and it is capitalized.

The example in the chart shows payments made under the Standard Repayment Plan (with a repayment period of 15 years based on the amount of the Direct Consolidation Loan) at an interest rate of 8.25%. In this example, you would pay $12 less per month and $2,150 less altogether if you pay the interest as it accrues during a 12-month deferment or forbearance period.

	If you pay the interest as it accrues...	If you do not pay the interest and it is capitalized...
Loan Amount	$15,000	$15,000
Interest for 12 Months	$1,238 (paid as accrued)	$1,238 (unpaid and capitalized)
Principal to be Repaid	$15,000	$16,238
Monthly Payment	$146	$158
Number of Payments	180	180
Total Repaid	$26,209	$28,359

Federal income tax deduction

You may be able to claim a federal income tax deduction for interest payments you make on Direct Loans. For further information, refer to IRS Publication 970, which is available at http://www.irs.ustreas.gov.

9. RESPONSIBILITY FOR PAYING ALL INTEREST ON ALL OR PART OF THE SUBSIDIZED PORTION OF A DIRECT CONSOLIDATION LOAN (FOR FIRST-TIME BORROWERS ON OR AFTER JULY 1, 2013)

If you were a **first-time borrower on or after July 1, 2013** (see Note below) when you received a Direct Subsidized Loan and you are now consolidating that loan, you may be responsible for paying the interest that accrues during all periods on the portion of your Direct Consolidation Loan that repaid the Direct Subsidized Loan, as explained below.

There is a limit on the maximum period of time (measured in academic years) for which a first-time borrower on or after July 1, 2013 can receive Direct Subsidized Loans. In general, a first-time borrower may not receive Direct Subsidized Loans for more than 150% of the published length of his or her program of study. This is called the "maximum eligibility period."

Generally, a first-time borrower on or after July 1, 2013 will become responsible for paying the interest that accrues during all periods on previously received Direct Subsidized Loans if the borrower:

- Continues to be enrolled in any undergraduate program after having received Direct Subsidized Loans for his or her maximum eligibility period, or
- Enrolls in another undergraduate program that is the same length as or shorter than the borrower's previous program.

There are a few exceptions to this rule. Your school or servicer can provide you with more information about this requirement and the exceptions.

You must pay the interest that accrues during all periods (including deferment periods) on the portion of your Direct Consolidation Loan that repaid a Direct Subsidized Loan you received as a first-time borrower on or after July 1, 2013 if:

- Before consolidating the Direct Subsidized Loan, you become responsible for paying all interest that accrues on that loan, as explained above; or
- After consolidating the Direct Subsidized Loan you become responsible for paying all interest that accrues on that loan, as explained above.

Note: A first-time borrower on or after July 1, 2013 is an individual who has no outstanding balance on a Direct Loan Program loan or a Federal Family Education Loan (FFEL) Program loan on July 1, 2013, or who has no outstanding balance on a Direct Loan or FFEL program loan on the date he or she obtains a Direct Loan Program loan after July 1, 2013.

10. REPAYMENT INCENTIVE PROGRAMS

A repayment incentive is a benefit that we offer to encourage you to repay your loan on time. The repayment incentive program described below may be available to you.

Interest rate reduction for automatic withdrawal of payments

Under the automatic withdrawal option, your bank automatically deducts your monthly loan payment from your checking or savings account and sends it to us. Automatic withdrawal helps to ensure that your payments are made on time. In addition, you receive a 0.25% interest rate reduction while you repay under the automatic withdrawal option. Your servicer will provide you with information about the automatic withdrawal option. You can also get the information on your servicer's web site, or by calling your servicer. Your servicer's web site address and toll-free telephone number are provided on correspondence that your servicer sends you.

Note: Another repayment incentive program, the up-front interest rebate, was available on Direct Subsidized Loans, Direct Unsubsidized Loans, and Direct PLUS Loans that were first disbursed before July 1, 2012. The rebate is equal to a percentage of the loan amount, and is the same amount that would result if the interest rate on the loan were lowered by a specific percentage. To permanently keep an up-front interest rebate, a borrower must make each of the first 12 required monthly payments on time when the loan enters repayment. If you consolidate a Direct Loan on which you received an up-front interest rebate before you have permanently earned

the rebate (the correspondence you received about your loan will tell you if you received a rebate), you will lose the rebate. The rebate amount will be added back to the principal balance of the loan before it is consolidated.

11. REPAYING YOUR LOAN

General

Unless you receive a deferment or forbearance on your loan (see Item 17), your first payment will be due within 60 days of the first disbursement of your Direct Consolidation Loan. Your servicer will notify you of the date your first payment is due.

You must make payments on your loan even if you do not receive a bill or repayment notice.

You must repay all of your Direct Loans under the same repayment plan, unless you want to repay your loans under the IBR Plan, the Pay As You Earn Plan, or the ICR Plan (see below) and you have other Direct Loans that do not qualify for repayment under those plans. In that case, you may select the IBR, Pay As You Earn, or ICR plan for the loans that are eligible for repayment under those plans, and may select a different repayment plan for the loans that may not be repaid under the IBR, Pay As You Earn, or ICR plan.

Repayment plans for all Direct Consolidation Loans

You may choose the Standard Repayment Plan, the Graduated Repayment Plan, the Extended Repayment Plan, or the Income-Contingent Repayment Plan to repay any Direct Consolidation Loan.

Standard Repayment Plan – Under this plan, you will make fixed monthly payments and repay your loan in full within 10 to 30 years (not including periods of deferment or forbearance) from the date the loan entered repayment, depending on the amount of your Direct Consolidation Loan and the amount of your other student loan debt (not to exceed the amount you are consolidating) as listed in the **Loans You Do Not Want to Consolidate** section of your Note (see the chart below). Your payments must be at least $50 a month ($600 a year) and will be more, if necessary, to repay the loan within the required time period.

Graduated Repayment Plan – Under this plan, you will usually make lower payments at first, and your payments will gradually increase over time. You will repay your loan in full within 10 to 30 years (not including periods of deferment or forbearance) from the date the loan entered repayment, depending on the total amount of your Direct Consolidation Loan and the amount of your other student loan debt (not to exceed the amount you are consolidating) as listed in **Loans You Do Not Want to Consolidate** section of your Note (see the chart below). Your monthly payment must at least be equal to the amount of interest that accrues each month. No single payment will be more than three times greater than any other payment.

Standard and Graduated Plans: Maximum Repayment Periods	
Total Education Loan Indebtedness	Maximum Repayment Period
Less than $7,500	10 years
$7,500 to $9,999	12 years
$10,000 to $19,999	15 years
$20,000 to $39,999	20 years
$40,000 to $59,999	25 years
$60,000 or more	30 years

Extended Repayment Plan – You are eligible for this plan only if: **(1)** you have an outstanding balance on Direct Loan Program Loans that exceeds $30,000; and **(2)** you had no outstanding balance on a Direct Loan Program loan as of October 7, 1998, or on the date you obtained a Direct Loan Program loan on or after October 7, 1998.

Under this plan, you will repay your loan in full over a repayment period not to exceed 25 years (not including periods of deferment or forbearance) from the date the loan entered repayment. You may choose to make fixed monthly payments or graduated monthly payments that start out lower and gradually increase over time. If you make fixed monthly payments, your payments must be at least $50 a month ($600 a year) and will be more, if necessary, to repay the loan within the required time period. If you make graduated monthly payments, you will usually make lower payments at first, and your payments will gradually increase over time. If you make graduated payments, your monthly payment must at least be equal to the amount of interest that accrues each month, and no single payment will be more than three times greater than any other payment.

Income-Contingent Repayment Plan (ICR Plan) – Under this plan, your monthly payment amount will be either 20% of your discretionary income or a percentage of what you would repay under a Standard Repayment Plan with a 12-year repayment period, whichever is less. Discretionary income for this plan is the difference between your adjusted gross income and the poverty guideline amount for your state of residence and family size. If you are married and file a joint federal income tax return, the income used to determine your ICR Plan payment amount will be the combined adjusted gross income of you and your spouse. Until we obtain the information needed to calculate your monthly payment amount, your payment will equal the amount of interest that accrues monthly on your loan unless you request a forbearance.

While you are repaying under the ICR Plan, you must annually provide documentation of your income and certify your family size. Your monthly payment amount may be adjusted annually based on the updated income and family size information that you provide.

Under the ICR Plan, if your loan is not repaid in full after you have made the equivalent of 25 years of qualifying monthly payments and at least 25 years have elapsed, any remaining loan amount will be forgiven. You may have to pay federal income tax on the loan amount that is forgiven.

Additional repayment plans for Direct Consolidation Loans that did not repay parent PLUS loans

In addition to the four repayment plans listed above that are available for any Direct Consolidation Loan, if you are not consolidating any parent Direct PLUS Loans or parent FFEL PLUS Loans you may also choose the **Income-Based Repayment Plan** or the **Pay As You Earn Repayment Plan** to repay your Direct Consolidation Loan. A parent PLUS loan is a PLUS loan that you obtained to help pay for your child's undergraduate education. You may not choose the Income-Based Repayment Plan or the Pay As You Earn Plan if you are consolidating a parent PLUS loan, but you may choose the Income-Contingent Repayment Plan (see above).

Income-Based Repayment Plan (IBR Plan) – Under the IBR Plan, your monthly payment amount is generally 15% (10% if you are a new borrower; see Note below) of your annual discretionary income, divided by 12. Discretionary income for this plan is the difference between your adjusted gross income and 150% of the poverty guideline amount for your state of residence and family size. If you are married and file a joint federal income tax return, the income used to determine your IBR Plan payment amount will be the combined adjusted gross income of you and your spouse.

To initially qualify for the IBR Plan and to continue to make payments that are based on your income, the amount you would be required to pay on your eligible student loans under the IBR Plan (as described above) must be less than the amount you would have to pay under the Standard Repayment Plan. If your IBR Plan payment amount is less than the amount you would have to pay under the Standard Repayment Plan, you are considered to have a "partial financial hardship."

If you are married and file a joint federal income tax return, the loan amount we use to determine whether you have a partial financial hardship will include your eligible loans and your spouse's eligible loans.

While you are repaying under the IBR Plan, you must annually provide documentation of your income and certify your family size so that we may determine whether you continue to have a partial financial hardship. Your monthly payment amount may be adjusted annually based on the updated income and family size information that you provide. If we determine that you no longer have a partial financial hardship, you may remain on the IBR Plan, but your monthly payment will no longer be based on your income. Instead, your monthly payment will be what you would be required to pay under the Standard Repayment Plan, based on the amount you owed on your eligible loans at the time you entered the IBR Plan.

Under the IBR Plan, if your loan is not repaid in full after you have made the equivalent of 25 years (20 years if you are a new borrower) of qualifying monthly payments and at least 25 years (20 years if you are a new borrower) have elapsed, any remaining loan amount will be forgiven. You may have to pay federal income tax on the loan amount that is forgiven.

Note: You are a **new borrower** for the IBR Plan if you have no outstanding balance on a Direct Loan Program or FFEL Program loan on July 1, 2014, or if you have no outstanding balance on a Direct Loan Program or FFEL Program loan on the date you obtain a Direct Loan Program loan after July 1, 2014. Your servicer will determine whether you are a new borrower based on the information about your loans in the U.S. Department of Education's National Student Loan Data System.

Pay As You Earn Repayment Plan (Pay As You Earn Plan) – Under the Pay As You Earn Plan, your monthly payment amount is generally 10% of your annual discretionary income, divided by 12. Discretionary income for this plan is the difference between your adjusted gross income and 150% of the poverty guideline amount for your state of residence and family size. If you are married and file a joint federal income tax return, the income used to determine your Pay As You Earn Plan payment amount will be the combined adjusted gross income of you and your spouse.

The Pay As You Earn Plan is available only to new borrowers. You are a new borrower for the Pay As You Earn Plan if:

1. You had no outstanding balance on a Direct Loan Program or FFEL Program loan as of October 1, 2007, or you have no outstanding balance on a Direct Loan Program or FFEL Program loan when you obtain a new loan on or after October 1, 2007, and

186

2. You receive a disbursement of a Direct Subsidized Loan, Direct Unsubsidized Loan, or student Direct PLUS Loan (a Direct PLUS Loan made to a graduate or professional student) on or after October 1, 2011, or you receive a Direct Consolidation Loan based on an application received on or after October 1, 2011. However, you are not considered to be a new borrower for the Pay As You Earn Plan if the Direct Consolidation Loan you receive repays loans that would make you ineligible under part 1 of this definition.

In addition to being a new borrower, to initially qualify for the Pay As You Earn Plan and to continue to make payments that are based on your income, the amount you would be required to pay on your eligible student loans under the Pay As You Earn Plan (as described above) must be less than the amount you would have to pay under the Standard Repayment Plan. If your Pay As You Earn Plan payment amount is less than the amount you would have to pay under the Standard Repayment Plan, you are considered to have a "partial financial hardship."

If you are married and file a joint federal income tax return, the loan amount we use to determine whether you have a partial financial hardship will include your eligible loans and your spouse's eligible loans.

While you are repaying under the Pay As You Earn Plan, you must annually provide documentation of your income and certify your family size so that we may determine whether you continue to have a partial financial hardship. Your monthly payment amount may be adjusted annually based on the updated income and family size information that you provide. If we determine that you no longer have a partial financial hardship, you may remain on the Pay As You Earn Plan, but your monthly payment will no longer be based on your income. Instead, your monthly payment will be what you would be required to pay under the Standard Repayment Plan, based on the amount you owed on your eligible loans at the time you entered the Pay As You Earn Plan.

Under the Pay As You Earn Plan, if your loan is not repaid in full after you have made the equivalent of 20 years of qualifying monthly payments and at least 20 years have elapsed, any remaining loan amount will be forgiven. You may have to pay federal income tax on the loan amount that is forgiven.

Additional repayment plan information

If you can show to our satisfaction that the terms and conditions of the repayment plans described above are not adequate to meet your exceptional circumstances, we may provide you with an alternative repayment plan.

If you do not choose a repayment plan, we will place you on the Standard Repayment Plan.

You may change repayment plans at any time after you have begun repaying your loan. There is no penalty if you make loan payments before they are due, or pay more than the amount due each month (prepayments).

We apply your payments made under any plan other than the IBR Plan and the Pay As You Earn Plan in the following order:

1. Late charges and collection costs,
2. Outstanding interest, and
3. Outstanding principal.

We apply your payments made under the IBR Plan or the Pay As You Earn Plan in the following order:

1. Outstanding interest,

2. Late charges and collection costs, and
3. Outstanding principal.

We apply any prepayments in accordance with the Act. Your servicer can provide more information about how prepayments are applied.

When you have repaid your loan in full, your servicer will send you a notice telling you that you have paid off your loan. You should keep this notice in a safe place.

12. TRANSFER OF LOAN

We may transfer the servicing of one or all of your loans to another servicer without your consent. If there is a change in the address to which you must send payments or direct communications, we will notify you of the new servicer's name, address and telephone number, the effective date of the transfer, and the date when you must begin sending payments or directing communications to that servicer. Transfer of a loan to a different servicer does not affect your rights and responsibilities under that loan.

13. LATE CHARGES AND COLLECTION COSTS

If you do not make any part of a payment within 30 days after it is due, we may require you to pay a late charge. This charge will not be more than six cents for each dollar of each late payment. If you do not make payments as scheduled, we may also require you to pay other charges and fees involved in collecting your loan.

14. DEMAND FOR IMMEDIATE REPAYMENT

The entire unpaid amount of your loan becomes due and payable (this is called "acceleration") if you:

- Make a false statement that causes you to receive a loan that you are not eligible to receive; or
- Default on your loan.

15. DEFAULTING ON YOUR LOAN

Default (failing to repay your loan) is defined in detail under "Acceleration and Default" in the **Note Terms and Conditions** section of this Note. If you default:

- We will require you to immediately repay the entire unpaid amount of your loan.
- We may sue you, take all or part of your federal and state tax refunds and other federal or state payments, and/or garnish your wages so that your employer is required to send us part of your salary to pay off your loan.
- We will require you to pay reasonable collection fees and costs, plus court costs and attorney fees.
- You will lose eligibility for other federal student aid and assistance under most federal benefit programs.
- You will lose eligibility for loan deferments.

We will report your default to nationwide consumer reporting agencies (see Item 16). This will harm your credit history and may make it difficult for you to obtain credit cards, home or car loans, or other forms of consumer credit.

16. CONSUMER REPORTING AGENCY NOTIFICATION

We will report information about your loan to nationwide consumer reporting agencies (commonly known as "credit bureaus") on a regular basis. This information will include the disbursement dates, amount, and repayment status of your loan (for example, whether you are current or delinquent in making payments). Your loan will be identified as an education loan.

If you default on a loan, we will report this to nationwide consumer reporting agencies. We will notify you at least 30 days in advance that we plan to report default information to a consumer reporting agency unless you resume making payments on the loan within 30 days of the date of the notice. You will be given a chance to ask for a review of the debt before we report it.

If a consumer reporting agency contacts us regarding objections you have raised about the accuracy or completeness of any information we have reported, we are required to provide the agency with a prompt response.

17. DEFERMENT AND FORBEARANCE (POSTPONING PAYMENTS)

General

If you meet certain requirements, you may receive a **deferment** that allows you to temporarily stop making payments on your loan.

If you cannot make your scheduled loan payments, but do not qualify for a deferment, we may give you a **forbearance**. A forbearance allows you to temporarily stop making payments on your loan, temporarily make smaller payments, or extend the time for making payments.

Deferment

You may receive a deferment:

- While you are enrolled at least half time at an eligible school;
- While you are in a full-time course of study in a graduate fellowship program;
- While you are in an approved full-time rehabilitation program for individuals with disabilities;
- While you are unemployed (for a maximum of three years; you must be diligently seeking, but unable to find, full-time employment);
- While you are experiencing an economic hardship (including Peace Corps service), as defined in the Act (for a maximum of three years);
- While you are serving on active duty during a war or other military operation or national emergency or performing qualifying National Guard duty during a war or other military operation or national emergency and, if you were serving on or after October 1, 2007, for an additional 180-day period following the demobilization date for your qualifying service; or
- If you are a member of the National Guard or other reserve component of the U.S. Armed Forces (current or retired) and you are called or ordered to active duty while you are enrolled at least half time at an eligible school or within 6 months of having been enrolled at least half time, during the 13 months following the conclusion of your active duty service, or until you return to enrolled student status on at least a half-time basis, whichever is earlier.

You may be eligible to receive additional deferments if, at the time you received your first Direct Loan, you had an outstanding balance on a loan made under the FFEL Program before July 1, 1993. If you meet this requirement, contact your servicer about additional deferments that may be available.

You may receive a deferment based on your enrollment in school on at least a half-time basis if:

1. You submit a deferment request to your servicer along with documentation of your eligibility for the deferment, or
2. Your servicer receives information from the school you are attending that indicates you are enrolled at least half time.

If your servicer processes a deferment based on information received from your school, you will be notified of the deferment and will have the option of canceling the deferment and continuing to make payments on your loan.

For all other deferments, you (or, for a deferment based on active duty military service or qualifying National Guard duty during a war or other military operation or national emergency, a representative acting on your behalf) must submit a deferment request to your servicer, along with documentation of your eligibility for the deferment. In certain circumstances, you may not be required to provide documentation of your eligibility if your servicer confirms that you have been granted the same deferment for the same period of time on a FFEL Program loan. Your servicer can provide you with a deferment request form that explains the eligibility and documentation requirements for the type of deferment you are requesting. You may also obtain deferment request forms and information on deferment eligibility requirements from your servicer's web site.

If you are in default on your loan, you are not eligible for a deferment.

You are not responsible for paying the interest on a Direct Subsidized Consolidation Loan during a period of deferment, except as explained in Item 9 of this Borrower's Rights and Responsibilities Statement. However, you are responsible for paying the interest on a Direct Unsubsidized Consolidation Loan during a period of deferment.

Forbearance

We may give you a forbearance if you are temporarily unable to make your scheduled loan payments for reasons including, but not limited to, financial hardship and illness.

We will give you a forbearance if:

- You are serving in a medical or dental internship or residency program, and you meet specific requirements;
- The total amount you owe each month for all of the student loans you received under Title IV of the Act (Direct Loan Program loans, FFEL Program loans, and Federal Perkins Loans) is 20% or more of your total monthly gross income (for a maximum of three years);
- You are serving in a national service position for which you receive a national service education award under the National and Community Service Act of 1993. In some cases, the interest that accrues on a qualified loan during the service period will be paid by the Corporation for National and Community Service;
- You are performing service that would qualify you for loan forgiveness under the Teacher Loan Forgiveness program that is available to certain Direct Loan and FFEL program borrowers;
- You qualify for partial repayment of your loans under a student loan repayment program administered by the Department of Defense; or
- You are called to active duty in the U.S. Armed Forces.

To request a forbearance, contact your servicer. Your servicer can explain the eligibility and documentation requirements for the type of forbearance you are requesting. You may also obtain information on forbearance eligibility requirements from your servicer's web site.

Under certain circumstances, we may also give you a forbearance without requiring you to submit a request or documentation. These circumstances include, but are not limited to, the following:

- Periods necessary for us to determine your eligibility for a loan discharge;

188

- A period of up to 60 days in order for us to collect and process documentation related to your request for a deferment, forbearance, change in repayment plan, or consolidation loan (we do not capitalize the interest that is charged during this period); or

- Periods when you are involved in a military mobilization, or a local or national emergency.

You are responsible for paying the interest that accrues on your entire Direct Consolidation Loan during a period of forbearance.

18. DISCHARGE (HAVING YOUR LOAN FORGIVEN)

Loan discharge due to death, bankruptcy, total and permanent disability, school closure, false certification, identity theft, or unpaid refund

We will discharge (forgive) your loan if:

- You die. Your servicer must receive acceptable documentation (as defined in the Act) of your death. We will also discharge the portion of a Direct Consolidation Loan that repaid one or more Direct PLUS Loans or Federal PLUS Loans obtained on behalf of a child who dies.

- Your loan is discharged in bankruptcy after you have proven to the bankruptcy court that repaying the loan would cause undue hardship. Direct Loans are not otherwise automatically discharged if you file for bankruptcy.

- You become totally and permanently disabled (as defined in the Act) and meet certain other requirements.

In certain cases, we may also discharge all or a portion of your loan if:

- One or more Direct Loan Program, FFEL Program, or Federal Perkins Loan Program loans that you consolidated was used to pay for a program of study that you (or the child for whom you borrowed a Direct PLUS Loan or Federal PLUS Loan) were unable to complete because the school closed;

- Your eligibility (or the eligibility of the child for whom you borrowed a Direct PLUS Loan or Federal PLUS Loan) for one or more of the Direct Loan Program or FFEL Program loans that you consolidated was falsely certified by the school;

- Your eligibility for one or more of the Direct Loan Program or FFEL Program loans that you consolidated was falsely certified as a result of a crime of identity theft; or

- The school did not pay a required refund of one or more Direct Loan Program or FFEL Program loans that you consolidated.

Teacher Loan Forgiveness

We may forgive a portion of your Direct Consolidation Loan that repaid Direct Subsidized Loans or Direct Unsubsidized Loans you received after October 1, 1998, or subsidized or unsubsidized Federal Stafford Loans you received under the FFEL program after October 1, 1998 if you:

- Teach full time for five consecutive years in certain low-income elementary or secondary schools, or for low-income educational service agencies;

- Meet certain other qualifications; and

- Did not owe a Direct Loan or a FFEL program loan as of October 1, 1998, or as of the date you obtain a loan after October 1, 1998.

Public Service Loan Forgiveness

A Public Service Loan Forgiveness program is also available. Under this program, we will forgive the remaining balance due on your eligible Direct Loan Program loans after you have made 120 payments on those loans

(after October 1, 2007) under certain repayment plans while you are employed full-time in certain public service jobs.

Additional loan discharge information

The Act may provide for certain loan forgiveness or repayment benefits on your loans in addition to the benefits described above. If other forgiveness or repayment options become available, your servicer will provide information about these benefits.

For a discharge based on your death or the death of the child on whose behalf you obtained a Direct PLUS Loan or Federal PLUS Loan that was consolidated, a family member must contact your loan servicer. To request a loan discharge based on one of the other conditions described above (except for a discharge due to bankruptcy), you must complete an application. Your servicer can tell you how to obtain an application.

In some cases, you may assert, as a defense against collection of your loan, that the school did something wrong or failed to do something that it should have done. You can make such a defense against repayment only if the school's act or omission directly relates to your loan or to the educational services that the loan was intended to pay for, and if what the school did or did not do would give rise to a legal cause of action against the school under applicable state law. If you believe that you have a defense against repayment of your loan, contact your servicer.

We do not guarantee the quality of the academic programs provided by schools that participate in federal student financial aid programs. You must repay your loan even if you do not complete your education, are unable to obtain employment in the field of study for which the school provided training, or are dissatisfied with, or do not receive, the education you paid for with the loan.

19. DEPARTMENT OF DEFENSE AND OTHER FEDERAL AGENCY LOAN REPAYMENT

Under certain circumstances, military personnel may have their federal education loans repaid by the Secretary of Defense. This benefit is offered as part of a recruitment program that does not apply to individuals based on their previous military service or to those who are not eligible for enlistment in the U.S. Armed Forces. For more information, contact your local military service recruitment office.

Other agencies of the federal government may also offer student loan repayment programs as an incentive to recruit and retain employees. Contact the agency's human resources department for more information.

END OF BORROWER'S RIGHTS AND RESPONSIBILITIES STATEMENT

ECONOMIC HARDSHIP DEFERMENT REQUEST

William D. Ford Federal Direct Loan (Direct Loan) Program / Federal Family Education Loan (FFEL) Program / Federal Perkins Loan (Perkins Loan) Program

OMB No. 1845-0011
Form Approved
Exp. Date 9/30/2018

HRD

WARNING: Any person who knowingly makes a false statement or misrepresentation on this form or on any accompanying document is subject to penalties that may include fines, imprisonment, or both, under the U.S. Criminal Code and 20 U.S.C. 1097.

SECTION 1: BORROWER INFORMATION

Please enter or correct the following information.

☐ **Check this box if any of your information has changed.**

SSN _____

Name _____

Address _____

City _____ State _____ Zip Code _____

Telephone - Primary _____

Telephone - Alternate _____

Email (Optional) _____

SECTION 2: BORROWER DETERMINATION OF DEFERMENT ELIGIBILITY

Carefully read the entire form before completing it. Complete Section 2 in its entirety. Maximum cumulative eligibility is 36 months per loan program. The federal student loan programs include the Direct Loan, FFEL, and Perkins Loan programs. For FFEL Program borrowers only, you are only eligible if all of your FFEL Program loans were first disbursed *one or after* July 1, 1993, or if you had no balance on a FFEL Program loan that was disbursed *before* July 1, 1993 when you received a loan *on or after* July 1, 1993. Instead of deferment, consider a repayment plan that determines your monthly payment amount based on your income. Visit **StudentAid.gov/IDR** for more information.

1. Have you been granted an Economic Hardship Deferment on a loan made under another federal student loan program for the same period of time for which you are applying for this deferment?

    For example, check "yes" if you are requesting deferment on your Direct Loans because you are on the deferment on your FFEL Program loans.

    ☐ Yes - Attach documentation of the deferment. Skip to Section 3.
    ☐ No - Continue to Item 2.

2. Have you received or are you receiving payments under a federal or state public assistance program that supports the period of time for which you are applying for this deferment?

    Qualifying programs include: Temporary Assistance for Needy Families (TANF), Supplemental Security Income (SSI), Supplemental Nutrition Assistance Program (SNAP), state general public assistance, or other means-tested benefits.

    ☐ Yes - Attach documentation of the payments. Skip to Section 3.
    ☐ No - Continue to Item 3.

3. Are you serving as a Peace Corps volunteer?

    ☐ Yes - Attach documentation certifying your period of service. Skip to Section 3.
    ☐ No - Continue to Item 4.

4. Do you work full time (see Section 5)?

    ☐ Yes - Continue to Item 5.
    ☐ No - You are not eligible for this deferment.

5. What is your monthly income? _____

    You must attach documentation of your monthly income. Monthly income is either (you choose):

    • Your gross income from all sources or

    • One-twelfth of the Adjusted Gross Income from your most recent federal income tax return.

6. What is your family size (see section 5)? _____

7. Is the amount you reported in Item 5 less than 150% of the poverty guideline for your family size and state of residence (see Table 2 in Section 5)?

    ☐ Yes - Continue to Section 3.
    ☐ No - You are not eligible for this deferment.

Borrower Name _____   Borrower SSN _____

SECTION 3: BORROWER REQUESTS, UNDERSTANDINGS, CERTIFICATIONS, AND AUTHORIZATION

I request:

- To defer repayment of my loans for the period during which I have an economic hardship, as described in Section 2.
- That my deferment begin on: _____
- ☐ If indicated, to make interest payments on my loans during my deferment.

I understand that:

- I am not required to make payments of loan principal or interest during my deferment.
- My deferment will begin on the later of the date I became eligible or the date that I requested.
- My deferment will end on the earlier of the date that I exhaust my maximum eligibility, the certified deferment end date, or when I am no longer eligible for the deferment for another reason.
- If I am a Perkins Loan borrower, I will receive a 6-month post-deferment grace period beginning on the date I no longer qualify for the deferment.
- Unless I am a Peace Corps volunteer, my deferment will be granted in increments of 1 year. If I continue to be eligible for an Economic Hardship Deferment after 1 year, I may reapply, subject to the cumulative maximum.
- Interest may capitalize on my loans during or at the expiration of my deferment or forbearance, but interest never capitalizes on Perkins Loans.

I certify that:

- The information I have provided on this form is true and correct.
- I will provide additional documentation to my loan holder, as required, to support my deferment eligibility.
- I will notify my loan holder immediately when my eligibility for the deferment ends.
- I have read, understand, and meet the eligibility requirements in Section 2.

I authorize the entity to which I submit this request and its agents to contact me regarding my request or my loans at any cellular telephone number that I provide now or in the future using automated telephone dialing equipment or artificial or prerecorded voice or text messages.

Borrower's Signature_____   Date _____

SECTION 4: INSTRUCTIONS FOR COMPLETING THE DEFERMENT REQUEST

Type or print using dark ink. Enter dates as month-day-year (mm-dd-yyyy). Example: March 14, 2015 = 03-14-2015. Include your name and account number on any documentation that you are required to submit with this form. If you want to apply for a deferment on loans that are held by different loan holders, you must submit a separate deferment request to each loan holder. **Return the completed form and any required documentation to the address shown in Section 6.**

SECTION 5: DEFINITIONS

Capitalization is the addition of unpaid interest to the principal balance of your loan. Capitalization causes more interest to accrue over the life of your loan and may cause your monthly payment amount to increase. Interest never capitalizes on Perkins Loans. Table 1 (below) provides an example of the monthly payments and the total amount repaid for a $30,000 unsubsidized loan.

The example loan has a 6% interest rate and the example deferment or forbearance lasts for 12 months and begins when the loan entered repayment. The example compares the effects of paying the interest as it accrues or allowing it to capitalize.

A **deferment** is a period during which you are entitled to postpone repayment of your loans. Interest is not generally charged to you during a deferment on your subsidized loans. Interest is always charged to you during a deferment on your unsubsidized loans. On loans made under the Perkins Loan Program, all deferments are followed by a post-deferment grace period of 6 months, during which time you are not required to make payments.

Family size includes **(1)** you, **(2)** your spouse, **(3)** your children if they receive more than half of their support from you, including unborn children who will be born during the deferment period, and **(4)** other people if, at the time you request this deferment, they live with you, receive more than half their support from you, and will continue to receive this support from you for the deferment period. Support includes money, gifts, loans, housing, food, clothes, car, medical and dental care, and payment of college costs.

The **Federal Family Education Loan (FFEL) Program** includes Federal Stafford Loans, Federal PLUS Loans, Federal Consolidation Loans, and Federal Supplemental Loans for Students (SLS).

The **Federal Perkins Loan (Perkins Loan) Program** includes Federal Perkins Loans, National Direct Student Loans (NDSL), and National Defense Student Loans (Defense Loans).

Full-time employment means working at least 30 hours per week in a position expected to last at least 3 consecutive months.

The **holder** of your Direct Loans is the Department. The holder of your FFEL Program loans may be a lender, guaranty agency, secondary market, or the Department. The holder of your Perkins Loans is an institution of higher education or the Department. Your loan holder may use a servicer to handle billing and other communications related to your loans. References to "your loan holder" on this form mean either your loan holder or your servicer.

A **subsidized loan** is a Direct Subsidized Loan, a Direct Subsidized Consolidation Loan, a Federal Subsidized Stafford Loan, portions of some Federal Consolidation Loans, Federal Perkins Loans, NDSL, and Defense Loans.

An **unsubsidized loan** is a Direct Unsubsidized Loan, a Direct Unsubsidized Consolidation Loan, a Direct PLUS Loan, a Federal Unsubsidized Stafford Loan, a Federal PLUS Loan, a Federal SLS, and portions of some Federal Consolidation Loans.

The **William D. Ford Federal Direct Loan (Direct Loan) Program** includes Federal Direct Stafford/Ford (Direct Subsidized) Loans, Federal Direct Unsubsidized Stafford/Ford (Direct Unsubsidized) Loans, Federal Direct PLUS (Direct PLUS) Loans, and Federal Direct Consolidation (Direct Consolidation) Loans.

Table 1. Capitalization Chart

Treatment of Interest with Deferment/Forbearance	Loan Amt.	Capitalized Interest	Outstanding Principal	Monthly Payment	Number of Payments	Total Repaid
Interest is paid	$30,000	$0	$30,000	$333	120	$41,767
Interest is capitalized at the end	$30,000	$1,800	$31,800	$353	120	$42,365
Interest is capitalized quarterly and at the end	$30,000	$1,841	$31,841	$354	120	$42,420

Table 2. 150% of the Poverty Guidelines for 2017 (Monthly)

Family Size	Alaska	Hawaii	All Others
1	$1,882.50	$1,732.50	$1,507.50
2	$2,536.25	$2,333.75	$2,030.00
3	$3,190.00	$2,935.00	$2,552.50
4	$3,843.75	$3,536.25	$3,075.00
5	$4,497.50	$4,137.50	$3,597.50
6	$5,151.25	$4,738.75	$4,120.00
7	$5,805.00	$5,340.00	$4,642.50
8	$6,458.75	$5,941.25	$5,165.00
Each add'l person, add	$653.75	$601.25	$522.50

If you do not live in the United States, use the poverty guideline amount in the column labeled "All Others".

SECTION 6: WHERE TO SEND THE COMPLETED DEFERMENT REQUEST

Return the completed form and any documentation to: (If no address is shown, return to your loan holder.)	If you need help completing this form, call: (If no phone number is shown, call your loan holder.)

SECTION 7: IMPORTANT NOTICES

Privacy Act Notice. The Privacy Act of 1974 (5 U.S.C. 552a) requires that the following notice be provided to you:

The authorities for collecting the requested information from and about you are §421 et seq., §451 et seq., or §461 of the Higher Education Act of 1965, as amended (20 U.S.C. 1071 et seq., 20 U.S.C. 1087a et seq., or 20 U.S.C. 1087aa et seq.) and the authorities for collecting and using your Social Security Number (SSN) are §§428B(f) and 484(a)(4) of the HEA (20 U.S.C. 1078-2(f) and 1091(a)(4)) and 31 U.S.C. 7701(b). Participating in the William D. Ford Federal Direct Loan (Direct Loan) Program, Federal Family Education Loan (FFEL) Program, or Federal Perkins Loan (Perkins Loan) Program and giving us your SSN are voluntary, but you must provide the requested information, including your SSN, to participate.

The principal purposes for collecting the information on this form, including your SSN, are to verify your identity, to determine your eligibility to receive a loan or a benefit on a loan (such as a deferment, forbearance, discharge, or forgiveness) under the Direct Loan, FFEL, or Federal Perkins Loan Programs, to permit the servicing of your loans, and, if it becomes necessary, to locate you and to collect and report on your loans if your loans become delinquent or default. We also use your SSN as an account identifier and to permit you to access your account information electronically.

The information in your file may be disclosed, on a case-by-case basis or under a computer matching program, to third parties as authorized under routine uses in the appropriate systems of records notices. The routine uses of this information include, but are not limited to, its disclosure to federal, state, or local agencies, to private parties such as relatives, present and former employers, business and personal associates, to consumer reporting agencies, to financial and educational institutions, and to guaranty agencies in order to verify your identity, to determine your eligibility to receive a loan or a benefit on a loan, to permit the servicing or collection of your loans, to enforce the terms of the loans, to investigate possible fraud and to verify compliance with federal student financial aid program regulations, or to locate you if you become delinquent in your loan payments or if you default. To provide default rate calculations, disclosures may be made to guaranty agencies, to financial and educational institutions, or to state agencies. To provide financial aid history information, disclosures may be made to educational institutions.

To assist program administrators with tracking refunds and cancellations, disclosures may be made to guaranty agencies, to financial and educational institutions, or to federal or state agencies. To provide a standardized method for educational institutions to efficiently submit student enrollment statuses, disclosures may be made to guaranty agencies or to financial and educational institutions. To counsel you in repayment efforts, disclosures may be made to guaranty agencies, to financial and educational institutions, or to federal, state, or local agencies.

In the event of litigation, we may send records to the Department of Justice, a court, adjudicative body, counsel, party, or witness if the disclosure is relevant and necessary to the litigation. If this information, either alone or with other information, indicates a potential violation of law, we may send it to the appropriate authority for action. We may send information to members of Congress if you ask them to help you with federal student aid questions. In circumstances involving employment complaints, grievances, or disciplinary actions, we may disclose relevant records to adjudicate or investigate the issues. If provided for by a collective bargaining agreement, we may disclose records to a labor organization recognized under 5 U.S.C. Chapter 71. Disclosures may be made to our contractors for the purpose of performing any programmatic function that requires disclosure of records. Before making any such disclosure, we will require the contractor to maintain Privacy Act safeguards. Disclosures may also be made to qualified researchers under Privacy Act safeguards.

Paperwork Reduction Notice. According to the Paperwork Reduction Act of 1995, no persons are required to respond to a collection of information unless such collection displays a valid OMB control number. The valid OMB control number for this information collection is 1845-0011. Public reporting burden for this collection of information is estimated to average 10 minutes per response, including time for reviewing instructions, searching existing data sources, gathering and maintaining the data needed, and completing and reviewing the collection of information. The obligation to respond to this collection is required to obtain a benefit in accordance with 34 CFR 674.34, 674.35, 674.36, 674.37, 682.210, or 685.204. If you have comments or concerns regarding the status of your individual submission of this form, please contact your loan holder directly (see Section 6).

LOAN DISCHARGE APPLICATION: SCHOOL CLOSURE

William D. Ford Federal Direct Loan (Direct Loan) Program, Federal Family Education Loan (FFEL) Program, and Federal Perkins Loan Program

OMB No. 1845-0058
Form Approved
Exp. Date 08/31/2017

WARNING: Any person who knowingly makes a false statement or misrepresentation on this form or on any accompanying document is subject to penalties that may include fines, imprisonment, or both, under the U.S. Criminal Code and 20 U.S.C. 1097.

SECTION 1: BORROWER IDENTIFICATION

Please enter or correct the following information.

☐ **Check this box if any of your information has changed.**

SSN ___ ___ ___ - ___ ___ - ___ ___ ___ ___

Name _____

Address _____

City, State, Zip Code _____

Telephone – Primary _____

Telephone – Alternate _____

E-mail (optional) _____

SECTION 2: SCHOOL CLOSURE INFORMATION

1. You are applying for this loan discharge as a:
   ☐ Student borrower – Skip to Item 4.
   ☐ Parent borrower – Continue to Item 2.

2. Student Name (Last, First, MI):
   _____

3. Student SSN:
   ___ ___ ___ - ___ ___ - ___ ___ ___ ___

4. Closed School Name:
   _____

5. Closed School Address (street, city, state, zip):
   _____

6. Dates of attendance at the closed school:
   _____ to _____

7. Name of the program you (or, for a parent PLUS borrower, the student) were enrolled in at the time the school closed:
   _____

8. Did you (or, for a parent PLUS borrower, the student) complete the program of study **at the closed school**?
   ☐ Yes – You are not eligible for this discharge.
   ☐ No – Continue to Item 9.

9. Were you (or for a parent PLUS borrower, the student) on an **approved** leave of absence when the school closed?
   ☐ Yes – Provide the dates of the leave of absence, then skip to Item 13:
   _____ to _____
   ☐ No – Continue to Item 10.

10. Were you (or, for a parent PLUS borrower, the student) still enrolled in the program of study when the school closed?
    ☐ Yes – Skip to Item 13.
    ☐ No – Continue to Item 11.

11. Did you (or, for a parent PLUS borrower, the student) withdraw from the school before the school closed?
    ☐ Yes – Continue to Item 12.
    ☐ No – Skip to Item 13.

12. On what date did you withdraw from the school?
    _____

13. Did you (or, for a parent PLUS borrower, the student) complete or are you in the process of completing the same or a comparable program of study at another school?
    ☐ Yes – Continue to Item 14.
    ☐ No – Skip to Item 16.

14. Are you (or, for a parent PLUS borrower, the student) completing the new program through a teach-out agreement (see Section 5)?
    ☐ Yes – You are not eligible for this discharge.
    ☐ No – Continue to Item 15.

15. Did the other school give you (or, for a parent PLUS borrower, the student) credit for training received at the closed school by allowing transfer credits or hours earned at the closed school, or by any other comparable means?
    ☐ Yes – You are not eligible for this discharge.
    ☐ No – Continue to Item 16.

194

Borrower Name: _____   Borrower SSN: __ __ __ - __ __ - __ __ __ __

SECTION 2: SCHOOL CLOSURE INFORMATION (CONTINUED)

16. Did the holder of your loan receive any money back (a refund) from the closed school on your behalf?

☐ Yes – Continue to Items 17–19.
☐ No – Skip to Item 19.
☐ Don't Know – Skip to Item 19.

17. What was the amount of the refund?
$ _____

18. Explain why the money was refunded:
_____
_____
_____

19. Did you (or, for a parent PLUS borrower, the student) make any monetary claim with, or receive any payment from, the closed school or any third party (see definition in Section 5) in connection with enrollment or attendance at the school?

☐ Yes – Continue to Items 20–22.
☐ No – Sign and date the form in Section 3. Submit the form to the loan holder in Section 7.
☐ Don't Know – Sign and date the form in Section 3. Submit the form to the loan holder in Section 7.

20. Provide the following about the party with whom the claim was made or from whom payment was received:

a. Name: _____

b. Address (street, city, state, zip code):
_____
_____

c. Telephone number:
_____

21. What is the amount and the status of the claim?
a. Amount: $ _____
b. Status: _____

22. What was the amount of any payment received? If none, write "none".
$ _____

Sign and date the form in Section 3. Submit the form to the loan holder in Section 7.

SECTION 3: BORROWER CERTIFICATIONS, ASSIGNMENT, AND AUTHORIZATION

▪ **I certify** that: **(1)** I received the Direct Loan, FFEL, or Perkins Loan Program loan funds directly, or as a credit that was applied to the amount owed to the school; **(2)** I (or, if I am a parent PLUS borrower, the student) was enrolled at the school identified in Section 2, was on an ***approved*** leave of absence on the date that the school closed, withdrew from the school not more than 120 days before it closed, or withdrew from the school more than 120 days before it closed if the Department determines that exceptional circumstances related to the school's closing justify an extension of this 120-day period (see Section 6); **(3)** Due to school closure, I (or, if I am a parent PLUS borrower, the student) did not complete the program of study at the closed school; **(4)** I (or, if I am a parent PLUS borrower, the student) did not complete and am not in the process of completing the program or a comparable program of study at the closed school at another school through a teach-out, by transferring credits or hours earned at the closed school to another school, or by any other comparable means; **(5)** I have read and agree to the terms and conditions for loan discharge, as specified in Section 6; **(6)** Under penalty of perjury, all of the information I have provided on this form and in any accompanying documentation is true and accurate to the best of my knowledge and belief.

▪ **I hereby assign and transfer** to the U.S. Department of Education (the Department) any right to a refund on the amount discharged that I may have received from the school identified in Section 2 of this form and/or any owners, affiliates, or assignees of the school, and from any third party that may pay claims for a refund because of the actions of the school, up to the amount discharged by the Department on my loan(s).

▪ **I authorize** the loan holder to which I submit this request (and its agents or contractors) to contact me regarding my request or my loan(s), including repayment of my loan(s), at the number that I provide on this form or any future number that I provide for my cellular telephone or other wireless device using automated telephone dialing equipment or artificial or prerecorded voice or text messages.

Borrower's Signature _____   Date _____

SECTION 4: INSTRUCTIONS FOR COMPLETING THE FORM

When completing this form, type or print using dark ink. Enter dates as month-day-year (mm-dd-yyyy). Use only numbers. Example: March 14, 2014 = 03-14-2014. If you need more space to answer any of the items, continue on separate sheets of paper and attach them to this form. Indicate the number of the Item(s) you are answering and include your name and Social Security Number (SSN) on the top of page 2 and on all attached pages. **Return the completed form and any attachments to the address shown in Section 7.**

SECTION 5: DEFINITIONS

- The **William D. Ford Federal Direct Loan (Direct Loan) Program** includes Federal Direct Stafford/Ford (Direct Subsidized) Loans, Federal Direct Unsubsidized Stafford/Ford (Direct Unsubsidized) Loans, Federal Direct PLUS (Direct PLUS) Loans, and Federal Direct Consolidation (Direct Consolidation) Loans.
- The **Federal Family Education Loan (FFEL) Program** includes Federal Stafford Loans (both subsidized and unsubsidized), Federal Supplemental Loans for Students (SLS), Federal PLUS Loans, and Federal Consolidation Loans.
- The **Federal Perkins Loan (Perkins Loan) Program** includes Federal Perkins Loans, National Direct Student Loans (NDSL), and National Defense Student Loans (Defense Loans).
- The **date a school closed** is the date that the school stopped providing educational instruction in *all programs* as determined by the Department.
- **Dates of attendance**: The "to" date means the last date that you (or, for a parent PLUS borrower, the student) actually attended the closed school.
- The **holder** of your Direct Loan Program loan(s) is the Department. The holder of your FFEL Program loan(s) may be a lender, a guaranty agency, or the Department. The holder of your Perkins Loan Program loans may be a school or the Department. Your loan holder may use a servicer to handle billing and other communications related to your loans. References to "your loan holder" on this form mean either your loan holder or your servicer.

- **Loan discharge** due to school closure cancels your obligation (and any endorser's obligation, if applicable) to repay the remaining portion on a Direct Loan, FFEL, or Perkins Program loan, and qualifies you for reimbursement of any amounts paid voluntarily or through forced collection on the loan. For consolidation loans, only the amount of the underlying loans that were used to pay for the program of study listed in Section 2 will be considered for discharge. The loan holder reports the discharge to all credit reporting agencies to which the holder previously reported the status of the loan and removes any adverse credit history previously associated with the loan.
- The **student** refers to the student for whom a parent borrower obtained a Direct PLUS Loan or Federal PLUS Loan.
- **Program of study** means the instructional program leading to a degree or certificate in which you (or, for parent PLUS borrowers, the student) were enrolled.
- **School** means the school's main campus, or any location or branch of the main campus.
- **Teach-out agreement** means a written agreement between schools that provides for the equitable treatment of students and a reasonable opportunity for students to complete their program of study if a school ceases to operate before all students have completed their program of study.
- **Third party** refers to any entity that may provide reimbursement for a refund owed by the closed school, such as a State or other entity offering a tuition recovery program or a holder of a performance bond.

SECTION 6: TERMS AND CONDITIONS FOR LOAN DISCHARGE BASED ON SCHOOL CLOSURE

- You are only eligible for this form of discharge if you received the loan on which you are requesting discharge on or after January 1, 1986.
- You are only eligible for this form of discharge if the location or campus that you were attending closed. If you were taking distance education classes, you are only eligible for discharge if the main campus of your school closed.
- You must have been enrolled at the closed school or on an approved leave of absence on the date that the school closed, or withdrawn from the school not more than 120 days before it closed to be eligible for this form of discharge.

- If you withdrew more than 120 days before the school closed, you may be eligible for this form of discharge if the Department determines that exceptional circumstances related to the school's closing justify an extension of this 120-day period. Examples of exceptional circumstances include, but are not limited to: **(1)** the closed school's loss of accreditation; **(2)** the closed school's discontinuation of the majority of its academic programs; **(3)** action by the State to revoke the closed school's license to operate or award academic credentials in the State; or **(4)** a finding by a State or Federal government agency that the closed school violated State or Federal law.

196

SECTION 6: TERMS AND CONDITIONS FOR LOAN DISCHARGE BASED ON SCHOOL CLOSURE (CONTINUED)

- By signing this form, you are agreeing to provide, upon request, testimony, a sworn statement, or other documentation reasonably available to you that demonstrates to the satisfaction of the Department or its designee that you meet the qualifications for loan discharge based on school closure, or that supports any representation that you made on this form or any accompanying documents.

- By signing this form, you are agreeing to cooperate with the Department or the Department's designee in any enforcement action related to this application.
- This application may be denied, or your discharge may be revoked, if you fail to provide testimony, a sworn statement, or documentation upon request, or if you provide testimony, a sworn statement, or documentation that does not support the material representation that you made on this form or on any accompanying documents.

SECTION 7: WHERE TO SEND THE COMPLETED FORM

Return the completed form and any required documentation to:
(If no address is shown, return to your loan holder.)

If you need help completing this form, call:
(If no telephone number is shown, call your loan holder.)

SECTION 8: IMPORTANT NOTICES

Privacy Act Notice. The Privacy Act of 1974 (5 U.S.C. 552a) requires that the following notice be provided to you:

The authorities for collecting the requested information from and about you are §421 *et seq.*, §451 *et seq.* and §461 *et seq.* of the Higher Education Act of 1965, as amended (20 U.S.C. 1071 *et seq.*, 20 U.S.C. 1087a *et seq.*, and 20 U.S.C. 1087aa *et seq.*) and the authorities for collecting and using your Social Security Number (SSN) are §§428B(f) and 484(a)(4) of the HEA (20 U.S.C. 1078-2(f) and 20 U.S.C. 1091(a)(4)) and 31 U.S.C. 7701(b). Participating in the William D. Ford Federal Direct Loan (Direct Loan) Program, the Federal Family Education Loan (FFEL) Program, or the Federal Perkins Loan (Perkins Loan) Program and giving us your SSN are voluntary, but you must provide the requested information, including your SSN, to participate.

The principal purposes for collecting the information on this form, including your SSN, are to verify your identity, to determine your eligibility to receive a loan or a benefit on a loan (such as a deferment, forbearance, discharge, or forgiveness) under the Direct Loan, FFEL, or Perkins Loan Programs, to permit the servicing of your loan(s), and, if it becomes necessary, to locate you and to collect and report on your loan(s) if your loan(s) becomes delinquent or defaults. We also use your SSN as an account identifier and to permit you to access your account information electronically.

The information in your file may be disclosed, on a case-by-case basis or under a computer matching program, to third parties as authorized under routine uses in the appropriate systems of records notices. The routine uses of this information include, but are not limited to, its disclosure to federal, state, or local agencies, to private parties such as relatives, present and former employers, business and personal associates, to consumer reporting agencies, to financial and educational institutions, and to guaranty agencies in order to verify your identity, to determine your eligibility to receive a loan or a benefit on a loan, to permit the servicing or collection of your loan(s), to enforce the terms of the loan(s), to investigate possible fraud and to verify compliance with federal student financial aid program regulations, or to locate you if you become delinquent in your loan payments or if you default. To provide default rate calculations, disclosures may be made to guaranty agencies, to financial and educational institutions, or to state agencies. To provide financial aid history information, disclosures may be made to educational institutions. To assist program administrators with tracking refunds and cancellations, disclosures may be made to guaranty agencies, to financial and educational institutions, or to federal or state agencies. To provide a standardized method for educational institutions to efficiently submit student enrollment statuses, disclosures may be made to guaranty agencies or to financial and educational institutions. To counsel you in repayment efforts, disclosures may be made to guaranty agencies, to financial and educational institutions, or to federal, state, or local agencies.

In the event of litigation, we may send records to the Department of Justice, a court, adjudicative body, counsel, party, or witness if the disclosure is relevant and necessary to the litigation. If this information, either alone or with other information, indicates a potential violation of law, we may send it to the appropriate authority for action. We may send information to members of Congress if you ask them to help you with federal student aid questions. In circumstances involving employment complaints, grievances, or disciplinary actions, we may disclose relevant records to adjudicate or investigate the issues. If provided for by a collective bargaining agreement, we may disclose records to a labor organization recognized under 5 U.S.C. Chapter 71. Disclosures may be made to our contractors for the purpose of performing any programmatic function that requires disclosure of records. Before making any such disclosure, we will require the contractor to maintain Privacy Act safeguards. Disclosures may also be made to qualified researchers under Privacy Act safeguards.

Paperwork Reduction Notice. According to the Paperwork Reduction Act of 1995, no persons are required to respond to a collection of information unless such collection displays a valid OMB control number. The valid OMB control number for this information collection is 1845-0058. Public reporting burden for this collection of information is estimated to average 30 minutes per response, including time for reviewing instructions, searching existing data sources, gathering and maintaining the data needed, and completing and reviewing the collection of information. The obligation to respond to this collection is required to obtain or retain a benefit (34 CFR 682.402(e)(3), or 685.215(c)). If you have comments or concerns regarding the status of your individual submission of this form, **contact your loan holder(s) (see Section 7) directly.**

DISCHARGE APPLICATION: TOTAL AND PERMANENT DISABILITY

William D. Ford Federal Direct Loan (Direct Loan) Program / Federal Family Education Loan (FFEL) Program / Federal Perkins Loan (Perkins Loan) Program / TEACH Grant Program

TPD-APP

OMB No. 1845-0065
Form Approved
Exp. Date 09/30/2019

This is an application for a total and permanent disability discharge of your Direct Loan, FFEL, and/or Perkins Loan program loan(s), and/or your Teacher Education Assistance for College and Higher Education (TEACH) Grant Program service obligation.

Throughout this application, the words "we," "us," and "our" refer to the U.S. Department of Education.

Make sure that Section 2, Section 3, and (if required) Section 4 include all requested information. Incomplete or inaccurate information may cause your application to be delayed or rejected.

To qualify for this discharge, you must submit documentation from **one** of the following sources:

1. The U.S. Department of Veterans Affairs (VA) **OR**
2. The Social Security Administration (SSA) **OR**
3. A physician's certification in Section 4 of this form

Except for VA or SSA determinations described below, a disability determination by another federal or state agency does not qualify you for this discharge.

U.S. Department of Veterans Affairs Documentation

If you are a veteran who has been determined by the VA to be unemployable due to a service-connected disability, you may qualify for discharge by providing documentation from the VA showing that you have received one of the following two types of VA disability determinations:

1. A determination that you have a service-connected disability (or disabilities) that is 100% disabling.
2. A determination that you are totally disabled based on an individual unemployability rating.

You do not qualify for discharge based on a VA disability determination if your disability is not service-connected.

Social Security Administration Documentation

If you are eligible for Social Security Disability Insurance (SSDI) or Supplemental Security Income (SSI), you may qualify for discharge by providing a copy of your notice of award or Benefits Planning Query (BPQY) from the SSA. You only qualify for a discharge based on this documentation if it shows that your next scheduled disability review will be 5 to 7 years or more from the date of your last SSA disability determination.

If you want to submit a BPQY but do not have one, contact the SSA office that issued your award and request form SSA-2459. You may also request a BPQY by calling 1-800-772-1213 or by visiting www.ssa.gov.

If you are granted a discharge based on SSA documentation, we will monitor your status during a 3-year monitoring period. Your discharged loans or TEACH Grant service obligation may be reinstated if you do not meet certain requirements, as explained in Section 6 of this form.

Physician Certification

You may qualify for discharge by having a physician complete Section 4 of this application. The physician must certify that you are unable to engage in any substantial gainful activity (see definition in Section 5) by reason of a medically determinable physical or mental impairment that:

1. Can be expected to result in death;
2. Has lasted for a continuous period of at least 60 months; or
3. Can be expected to last for a continuous period of at least 60 months.

If you are granted a discharge based on a physician's certification, we will monitor your status during a 3-year monitoring period. Your discharged loans or TEACH Grant service obligation may be reinstated if you do not meet certain requirements, as explained in Section 6 of this form.

Important Tax Information

Loan amounts discharged due to total and permanent disability may be considered taxable income by the Internal Revenue Service (IRS). Contact the IRS for more information.

How to Designate Someone to Represent You

If you wish to designate an individual or organization to represent you in matters related to your total and permanent disability discharge request, you must complete the Applicant Representative Designation: Total and Permanent Disability form. You may obtain this form from our Total and Permanent Disability Discharge Servicer (see below for contact information).

WHERE TO SEND YOUR COMPLETED APPLICATION AND DOCUMENTATION

U.S. Department of Education - TPD Servicing
P.O. Box 87130
Lincoln, NE 68501-7130
Fax: 303-696-5250

IF YOU NEED HELP COMPLETING THE APPLICATION

Phone: 1-888-303-7818 (TTY: dial 711, then phone no.)
Email: disabilityinformation@nelnet.com
Website: www.disabilitydischarge.com

Page 1 of 8

DISCHARGE APPLICATION: TOTAL AND PERMANENT DISABILITY

William D. Ford Federal Direct Loan (Direct Loan) Program / Federal Family Education Loan (FFEL) Program / Federal Perkins Loan (Perkins Loan) Program / TEACH Grant Program

TPD-APP

OMB No. 1845-0065
Form Approved
Exp. Date 09/30/2019

WARNING: Any person who knowingly makes a false statement or misrepresentation on this form or on any accompanying document is subject to penalties that may include fines, imprisonment, or both, under the U.S. Criminal Code and 20 U.S.C. 1097.

SECTION 1: APPLICANT INFORMATION

Please enter or correct the following information.

☐ **Check this box if any of your information has changed.**

SSN	_____
Date of Birth	_____
Name	_____
Address	_____
City	_____ State _____ Zip Code _____
Telephone - Primary	_____
Telephone - Alternate	_____
Email (Optional)	_____

SECTION 2: TOTAL AND PERMANENT DISABILITY INFORMATION

Carefully read the entire application. Type or print in dark ink. Sign and date the application in Section 3.

1. Are you a veteran who has received a determination from the U.S. Department of Veterans Affairs (VA) that you are **unemployable due to a service-connected disability?**
   ☐ Yes - Attach documentation of the VA determination and complete Section 3. You do not need to have a physician complete Section 4.
   ☐ No - Continue to Item 2.

2. Are you currently receiving SSDI or SSI benefits, and does your most recent notice of award of Benefits Planning Query (BPQY) from the SSA state that **your next scheduled disability review will be 5 to 7 years or more from the date of your last SSA disability determination?**
   ☐ Yes - Attach a copy of your most recent SSA notice of award or BPQY and complete Section 3. You do not need to have a physician complete Section 4.
   ☐ No - Complete Section 3 and have a physician complete and sign Section 4.

SECTION 3: APPLICANT'S REQUEST, AUTHORIZATION, UNDERSTANDINGS, AND CERTIFICATIONS

I request that the U.S. Department of Education discharge my Direct Loan, FFEL, and/or Perkins Loan program loan(s), and/or my TEACH Grant service obligation.

I authorize any physician, hospital, or other institution having records about the disability that is the basis for my request for a discharge to make information from those records available to the U.S. Department of Education.

I understand that:

1. If I am applying for a discharge based on a physician's certification in Section 4, **I must submit this application to the U.S. Department of Education within 90 days of the date of my physician's signature in Section 4.**

2. If I am a veteran who answered No to Item 1 in Section 2, and I obtained a certification from a physician in Section 4, that certification is only for purposes of determining my eligibility for a discharge of my loan(s) or TEACH Grant service obligation, and is not for purposes of determining my eligibility for, or the extent of my eligibility for, VA benefits.

I certify that: **(1)** I have a total and permanent disability, as defined in Section 5; and **(2)** I have read and understand the information in Sections 6 and 7.

_____   _____   **Representative Name (if applicable)**
Applicant's or Representative's Signature   **Date**

NOTE: You may designate someone to represent you in matters related to your application. If you wish to designate a representative, you must complete the Applicant Representative Designation: Total and Permanent Disability form.

Page 2 of 8

200

SECTION 4: PHYSICIAN'S CERTIFICATION

Print legibly and initial any changes. Return the form to the applicant or representative.

Applicant Identification

1. Provide the below information regarding the individual for whom you are completing this Section:

   Name _____

   Date of Birth _____

Medically Determinable Physical or Mental Impairment

2. Does the applicant have a medically determinable physical or mental impairment that prevents the applicant from engaging in any substantial gainful activity?

   Substantial gainful activity means a level of work performed for pay or profit that involves doing significant physical or mental activities or a combination of both. If the applicant is able to engage in any substantial gainful activity in any field of work, you must answer "No".

   ☐ Yes - Continue to Item 3.

   ☐ No - **Do not complete this application.**

Severity/Duration of Physical or Mental Impairment

3. Is the applicant's impairment expected to result in death?

   ☐ Yes - Skip to Item 5.

   ☐ No - Continue to Item 4.

4. Has the applicant's impairment lasted or is it expected to last for a continuous period of at least 60 months?

   ☐ Yes - Continue to Item 5.

   ☐ No - **Do not complete this application.**

Disabling Condition

Do not use insurance codes or abbreviations.

5. Provide your diagnosis of the applicant's impairment:

6. Describe the severity of the applicant's impairment, including, if applicable, the phase of the impairment:

Limitations

Explain how the condition prevents the applicant from engaging in any substantial gainful activity in any field of work. Attach additional pages if needed. Enter "N/A" if not applicable. You may include additional information you believe is helpful in understanding the applicant's condition, such as medications or procedures used to treat the condition.

7. Limitations on sitting, standing, walking, or lifting:

8. Limitations on activities of daily living:

9. Residual functionality:

10. Social/behavioral limitations (if any):

11. Global Assessment Function Score (for psychiatric conditions):

Physician's Certification

I certify that, in my best professional judgment, the applicant identified in Item 1 has a medically determinable physical or mental impairment consistent with my responses in Items 2 through 10.

I understand that an applicant who is currently able to engage in any substantial gainful activity in any field of work does not have a total and permanent disability as defined on this form.

I am a doctor of: ☐ medicine ☐ osteopathy/osteopathic medicine

_____ State Where Legally Authorized to Practice*   _____ Professional License Number (subject to verification; stamp is acceptable)

*If you are licensed to practice in American Samoa, Puerto Rico, the U.S. Virgin Islands, the Northern Mariana Islands, the Marshall Islands, Micronesia, or Palau, attach a copy of your professional license that clearly shows the expiration date.

_____ Physician's Signature (a stamp is not acceptable)   _____ Date (mm-dd-yyyy)   **Physician Name (First, Middle, Last)**

_____ Email   _____ Telephone

_____ Address (a stamp is acceptable)

_____ Fax

SECTION 5: DEFINITIONS

If you have a **total and permanent disability**, this means that: **(1)** you are unable to engage in any substantial gainful activity by reason of a medically determinable physical or mental impairment that can be expected to result in death, or that has lasted for a continuous period of not less than 60 months, or that can be expected to last for a continuous period of not less than 60 months; **OR (2)** you are a veteran who has been determined by the VA to be unemployable due to a service-connected disability. Except for certain individuals who have received SSA notices of award for SSDI or SSI benefits, or for certain veterans, a disability determination by another federal or state agency does not establish your eligibility for a discharge of your loan(s) and/or TEACH Grant service obligation due to a total and permanent disability.

Substantial gainful activity means a level of work performed for pay or profit that involves doing significant physical or mental activities, or a combination of both.

A **discharge of a loan** due to a total and permanent disability cancels your obligation (and, if applicable, an endorser's obligation) to repay the remaining balance on your Direct Loan, FFEL, and/or Perkins Loan program loans. A **discharge of a TEACH Grant service obligation** cancels your obligation to complete the teaching service that you agreed to perform as a condition for receiving a TEACH Grant.

The **post-discharge monitoring period** begins on the date we grant a discharge of your loan(s) or TEACH Grant service obligation and lasts for three years. If you fail to meet certain conditions at any time during or at the end of the post-discharge monitoring period, we will reinstate your obligation to repay your loan(s) or complete your TEACH Grant service. See Section 6 for more information.

Note to Veterans: The post-discharge monitoring period does not apply if you are a veteran who receives a discharge based on a determination from the VA that you are unemployable due to a service-connected disability.

The **William D. Ford Federal Direct Loan (Direct Loan) Program** includes Federal Direct Stafford/Ford Loans (Direct Subsidized Loans), Federal Direct Unsubsidized Stafford/Ford Loans (Direct Unsubsidized Loans), Federal Direct PLUS Loans (Direct PLUS Loans), and Federal Direct Consolidation Loans (Direct Consolidation Loans).

The **Federal Family Education Loan (FFEL) Program** includes Federal Stafford Loans (both subsidized and unsubsidized), Federal Supplemental Loans for Students (SLS), Federal PLUS Loans, and Federal Consolidation Loans.

The **Federal Perkins Loan (Perkins Loan) Program** includes Federal Perkins Loans, National Direct Student Loans (NDSL), and National Defense Student Loans (Defense Loans).

The **Teacher Education Assistance for College and Higher Education (TEACH) Grant Program** requires individuals to complete a teaching service obligation as a condition for receiving a TEACH Grant.

The **holder** of your FFEL Program loan(s) may be a lender, a guaranty agency, or the U.S. Department of Education. The holder of your Perkins Loan Program loan(s) may be a school you attended or the U.S. Department of Education. The holder of your Direct Loan Program loan(s) and/or your TEACH Grant Agreement to Serve (if you received a TEACH Grant) is the U.S. Department of Education. Your loan holder may use a servicer to handle billing and other matters related to your loan. The term "holder" as used on this application means either your loan holder or, if applicable, your loan servicer.

The term **"state"** for purposes of the physician's certification in Section 4 (the physician must be licensed to practice in a state) includes the 50 United States, the District of Columbia, American Samoa, the Commonwealth of Puerto Rico, Guam, the U.S. Virgin Islands, the Commonwealth of the Northern Mariana Islands, the Republic of the Marshall Islands, the Federated States of Micronesia, and the Republic of Palau.

A **representative** is a member of your family, your attorney, a law firm or legal aid society, or another individual or organization authorized to act on your behalf in connection with your total and permanent disability discharge application.

SECTION 6: DISCHARGE PROCESS / ELIGIBILITY REQUIREMENTS / TERMS AND CONDITIONS FOR DISCHARGE

Applying for discharge (all applicants):

Submission of discharge application. After you submit your completed application and documentation to us, we will send you a notice that will:

- Acknowledge receipt of your application;
- Explain the process for our review of your application; and
- Inform you that you are not required to make any payments on your loans while we review your application for discharge.

Consequences of failure to submit an application. If you do not submit an application to us within 120 days of notifying us that you intend to submit an application, collection activity will resume on your loans, and your loan holder may capitalize any unpaid interest. This means that the unpaid interest will be added to the principal balance of your loans, and interest will then be charged on the increased loan principal amount. However, if you have a FFEL Program loan and the loan holder is a guaranty agency, or if you have a Federal Perkins Loan, unpaid interest will not be capitalized.

Discharge process for veterans who have been determined by the VA to be unemployable due to a service-connected disability:

Our review of your discharge application. We will review the documentation from the VA to determine if you are totally and permanently disabled as described in item **(2)** of the definition of "total and permanent disability" in Section 5 of this application.

Determination of eligibility or ineligibility for discharge. If we determine that you are totally and permanently disabled, you will be notified that your loans and/or TEACH Grant service obligation has been discharged. The discharge will be reported to nationwide consumer reporting agencies, and any loan payments received on your loan on or after the effective date of the determination by the VA that you are unemployable due to a service-connected disability will be refunded to the person who made the payments.

If we determine that you are **not** totally and permanently disabled, you will be notified of that determination. The notification will include:

- The reason or reasons for the denial of your discharge application;

- An explanation that your loans are due and payable to the loan holder under the terms of the promissory note that you signed and that your loans will return to the status they were in at the time you applied for a total and permanent disability discharge;

- An explanation that your loan holder will notify you of the date that you must resume making payments on your loans; and

- An explanation that if you applied for a discharge of a TEACH Grant service obligation, you must comply with all terms and conditions of your TEACH Grant Agreement to Serve.

The notification will also explain your ability to request reconsideration of this determination or to submit a new discharge application:

- You may request that we re-evaluate your discharge application by providing additional documentation from the VA that supports your eligibility for discharge. If you provide this documentation within 12 months of the date of our notification that you are ineligible for discharge, you do not have to submit a new application. After 12 months, a new application is required.

- If the documentation from the VA does not indicate that you are unemployable due to a service-connected disability, you may reapply for discharge under the "Discharge Process For All Other Applicants". You must submit a new application with the required documentation from the SSA or a physician's certification in Section 4.

Discharge process for all other applicants:

Our review of your discharge application. If you submit a discharge application supported by an award of benefits notice from the SSA or an SSA Benefits Planning Query (BPQY), we will review that documentation to determine if it meets the requirements described in Section 2, Item 2 of this form.

If you submit a discharge application supported by a physician's certification in Section 4 of this application, we will review the physician's certification and any accompanying documentation to determine if you are totally and permanently disabled as described in item **(1)** of the definition of "total and permanent disability" in Section 5 of this application. We may also contact your physician for additional information, or may arrange for an additional review of your condition by an independent physician at our expense. Based on the results of this review, we will determine your eligibility for discharge.

If we determine during our review of your application that you received a Direct Loan or Perkins Loan program loan, or a TEACH Grant before the date we received the SSA notice of award (or BPQY) or before the date the physician certified your application in Section 4, and a disbursement of that loan or grant is made after that date, but before we have granted a discharge, we will suspend processing of your discharge request until you ensure that the full amount of the disbursement is returned to the loan holder or (for a TEACH Grant) to us.

If you apply for a total and permanent disability discharge and we determine as part of our review that a new Direct Loan or Perkins Loan program loan or a new TEACH Grant was made to you on or after the date we received the SSA notice of award (or BPQY) or the date the physician certified your application in Section 4, and before the date we grant a discharge, we will deny your discharge request. Collection will resume on your loans and you will again be responsible for complying with the terms and conditions of your TEACH Grant Agreement to Serve.

Determination of eligibility or ineligibility for discharge. If we determine that you are totally and permanently disabled, we will notify you that a discharge has been approved, and that you will be subject to a post-discharge monitoring period for three years beginning on the discharge date. The notification of discharge will explain the terms and conditions under which we will reinstate your obligation to repay your loan or to complete your TEACH service. The discharge will be reported to nationwide consumer reporting agencies, and any loan payments that were received after the date we received the SSA notice of award (or BPQY) or after the date the physician certified your discharge application will be returned to the person who made the payments.

Discharge process for all other applicants (continued):

Determination of eligibility or ineligibility for discharge (continued).

If we determine that you are **not** totally and permanently disabled, you will be notified of that determination. The notification will include:

- The reason or reasons for the denial of your discharge application;

- An explanation that your loans are due and payable to the loan holder under the terms of the promissory note that you signed and that your loans will return to the status that would have existed if your total and permanent disability discharge application had not been received;

- An explanation that your loan holder will notify you of the date you must resume making payments on your loans;

- An explanation that if you applied for a discharge of a TEACH Grant service obligation, you must comply with all terms and conditions of your TEACH Grant Agreement to Serve;

- An explanation that you are not required to submit a new total and permanent disability discharge application if, within 12 months of the date of our notification to you that you are ineligible for discharge, you provide additional information regarding your disabling condition that supports your eligibility for discharge, and you request that we re-evaluate your discharge application; and

- An explanation that if you do not request re-evaluation of your prior discharge application within 12 months of the date of our notification of ineligibility for discharge, and you still wish to have us re-evaluate your eligibility for a total and permanent disability discharge, you must submit a new total and permanent disability discharge application to us.

- If you request a re-evaluation of your total and permanent disability discharge application or submit a new total and permanent disability discharge application, as described above, your request must include new information regarding your disabling condition that was not provided to us in connection with your prior application for discharge.

Post-discharge monitoring period. If you are granted a discharge, we will monitor your status during the 3-year post-discharge monitoring period that begins on the date the discharge is granted.

We will reinstate the requirement for you to repay your loans and/or complete your TEACH Grant service if, at any time during or at the end of the post-discharge monitoring period, you:

- Receive annual earnings from employment that exceed the poverty guideline amount (see **Note** below) for a family of two in your state, regardless of your actual family size;

- Receive a new loan under the Direct Loan Program or the Perkins Loan Program, or a new TEACH Grant;

- Receive a disbursement of a Direct Loan Program or Perkins Loan Program loan or a TEACH Grant that was initially disbursed prior to your discharge date and you fail to ensure that the disbursement is returned to the loan holder or (for a TEACH Grant) to us within 120 days of the disbursement date; or

- Receive a notice from the SSA indicating that you are no longer disabled or that your continuing disability review will no longer be the 5- to 7-year period indicated in the SSA notice of award or BPQY.

During the 3-year post-discharge monitoring period, you (or your representative) must:

- Promptly notify us of any changes in your address or telephone number;

- Promptly notify us if your annual earnings from employment exceed the poverty guideline amount for a family of two in your state (see **Note** below), regardless of your actual family size;

- Upon request, provide us with documentation of your annual earnings from employment, on a form that we will provide; and

- Promptly notify us if you receive a notice from the SSA indicating that you are no longer disabled or that your continuing disability review will no longer be the 5- to 7-year period indicated in the SSA notice of award or BPQY (after you had been previously determined to be disabled by the SSA, were receiving SSDI or SSI benefits, and had a continuing disability review period of 5 to 7 years or more from the date of your last SSA disability determination).

Note: The poverty guideline amounts are updated annually and may be obtained at **http://aspe.hhs.gov/poverty**. We will notify you of the current poverty guideline amounts during each year of the post-discharge monitoring period.

Discharge process for all other applicants (continued):

Reinstatement of obligation to repay discharged loans or complete discharged TEACH Grant service obligation. If you do not meet the requirements described above at any time during or at the end of the post-discharge monitoring period, we will reinstate your obligation to repay your loans and/or to complete your TEACH Grant service. If your loans are reinstated, you will be responsible for repaying your loans to us in accordance with the terms of your promissory note(s). Your loans will be returned to the status that would have existed if we had not received your total and permanent disability discharge application. However, you will not be required to pay interest on your loans for the period from the date of the discharge until the date your repayment obligation was reinstated. We will be your loan holder. If your TEACH Grant service obligation is reinstated, you will again be subject to the requirements of your TEACH Grant Agreement to Serve. If you do not meet the terms of that agreement and the TEACH Grant funds you received are converted to a Direct Unsubsidized Loan, you must repay that loan in full, and interest will be charged from the date(s) that the TEACH Grant funds were disbursed.

If your obligation to repay your loans or to complete your TEACH Grant service is reinstated, we will notify you of the reinstatement. This notification will include:

- The reason or reasons for the reinstatement;
- For loans, an explanation that the first payment due date on the loan following the reinstatement will be no earlier than 60 days following the date of the notification of reinstatement; and
- Information on how you may contact us if you have questions about the reinstatement, or if you believe that your obligation to repay a loan or complete TEACH Grant service was reinstated based on incorrect information.

SECTION 7: ELIGIBILITY REQUIREMENTS TO RECEIVE FUTURE LOANS OR TEACH GRANTS

For veterans who receive a total and permanent disability discharge based on a determination by the VA that they are unemployable due to a service-connected disability:

If you are a veteran who is granted a **discharge** based on a determination that you are totally and permanently disabled as described in item **(2)** of the definition of "total and permanent disability" in Section 5 of this application, you are not eligible to receive future loans under the Direct Loan Program or the Perkins Loan Program, or future TEACH Grants, unless:

- You obtain a certification from a physician that you are able to engage in substantial gainful activity; and
- You sign a statement acknowledging that the new loan or TEACH Grant service obligation cannot be discharged in the future on the basis of any injury or illness present at the time the new loan or TEACH Grant is made, unless your condition substantially deteriorates so that you are again totally and permanently disabled.

For all other individuals who receive a total and permanent disability discharge:

If you are granted a **discharge** based on a determination that you are totally and permanently disabled in accordance with item **(1)** of the definition of "total and permanent disability" in Section 5 of this application, you are not eligible to receive future loans under the Direct Loan Program or the Perkins Loan Program, or future TEACH Grants, unless:

- You obtain a certification from a physician that you are able to engage in substantial gainful activity;
- You sign a statement acknowledging that the new loan or TEACH Grant service obligation cannot be discharged in the future on the basis of any injury or illness present at the time the new loan or TEACH Grant is made, unless your condition substantially deteriorates so that you are again totally and permanently disabled; and
- If you request a Direct Loan Program or Perkins Loan Program loan, or a new TEACH Grant, within three years of the date that a previous loan or TEACH Grant was discharged, you resume payment on the previously discharged loan or acknowledge that you are once again subject to the terms of the TEACH Grant Agreement to Serve before receiving the new loan.

SECTION 8: WHERE TO SEND THE COMPLETED DISCHARGE APPLICATION

Return the completed form and any documentation to:

U.S. Department of Education - TPD Servicing
P.O. Box 87130
Lincoln, NE 68501-7130
Fax to: 303-696-5250
Email to: disabilityinformation@nelnet.com

If you need help completing this form, contact us:

Phone: 1-888-303-7818 (TTY: dial 771, then phone no.)
Email: disabilityinformation@nelnet.com
Website: www.disabilitydischarge.com

SECTION 9: IMPORTANT NOTICES

Privacy Act Notice. The Privacy Act of 1974 (5 U.S.C. 552a) requires that the following notice be provided to you:

The authorities for collecting the requested information from and about you are §421 et seq., §451 et seq., §461, or §420L of the Higher Education Act of 1965, as amended (20 U.S.C. 1071 et seq., 20 U.S.C. 1087a et seq., 20 U.S.C. 1087aa et seq., or 20 U.S.C. 1070g et seq.) and the authorities for collecting and using your Social Security Number (SSN) are §§428B(f) and 484(a)(4) of the HEA (20 U.S.C. 1078-2(f) and 1091(a)(4)) and 31 U.S.C. 7701(b). Participating in the Direct Loan,FFEL, Perkins Loan, or TEACH Grant program and giving us your SSN are voluntary, but you must provide the requested information, including your SSN, to participate.

The principal purposes for collecting the information on this form, including your SSN, are to verify your identity, to determine your eligibility to receive a loan or a benefit on a loan (such as a deferment, forbearance, discharge, or forgiveness) under the Direct Loan, FFEL, Federal Perkins Loan or TEACH Grant Programs, to permit the servicing of your loans, and, if it becomes necessary, to locate you and to collect and report on your loans if your loans become delinquent or default. We also use your SSN as an account identifier and to permit you to access your account information electronically.

The information in your file may be disclosed, on a case-by-case basis or under a computer matching program, to third parties as authorized under routine uses in the appropriate systems of records notices. The routine uses of this information include, but are not limited to, its disclosure to federal, state, or local agencies, to private parties such as relatives, present and former employers, business and personal associates, to consumer reporting agencies, to financial and educational institutions, and to guaranty agencies in order to verify your identity, to determine your eligibility to receive a loan or a benefit on a loan, to permit the servicing or collection of your loans, to enforce the terms of the loans, to investigate possible fraud and to verify compliance with federal student financial aid program regulations, or to locate you if you become delinquent in your loan payments or if you default. To provide default rate calculations, disclosures may be made to guaranty agencies, to financial and educational institutions, or to state agencies. To provide financial aid history information, disclosures may be made to educational institutions.

To assist program administrators with tracking refunds and cancellations, disclosures may be made to guaranty agencies, to financial and educational institutions, or to federal or state agencies. To provide a standardized method for educational institutions to efficiently submit student enrollment statuses, disclosures may be made to guaranty agencies or to financial and educational institutions. To counsel you in repayment efforts, disclosures may be made to guaranty agencies, to financial and educational institutions, or to federal, state, or local agencies.

In the event of litigation, we may send records to the Department of Justice, a court, adjudicative body, counsel, party, or witness if the disclosure is relevant and necessary to the litigation. If this information, either alone or with other information, indicates a potential violation of law, we may send it to the appropriate authority for action. We may send information to members of Congress if you ask them to help you with federal student aid questions. In circumstances involving employment complaints, grievances, or disciplinary actions, we may disclose relevant records to adjudicate or investigate the issues. If provided for by a collective bargaining agreement, we may disclose records to a labor organization recognized under 5 U.S.C. Chapter 71. Disclosures may be made to our contractors for the purpose of performing any programmatic function that requires disclosure of records. Before making any such disclosure, we will require the contractor to maintain Privacy Act safeguards. Disclosures may also be made to qualified researchers under Privacy Act safeguards.

Paperwork Reduction Notice. According to the Paperwork Reduction Act of 1995, no persons are required to respond to a collection of information unless such collection displays a valid OMB control number. The valid OMB control number for this information collection is 1845-0065. Public reporting burden for this collection of information is estimated to average 30 minutes per response, including time for reviewing instructions, searching existing data sources, gathering and maintaining the data needed, and completing and reviewing the collection of information. The obligation to respond to this collection is required to obtain a benefit in accordance with 34 CFR 674.61(b) or (c), 34 CFR 682.402(c)(2) or (c)(9), 34 CFR 685.213(b) or (c), and 34 CFR 686.42(b). If you have comments or concerns regarding the status of your individual submission of this form, please contact the U.S. Department of Education directly (see Section 6).

Form 8857
(Rev. January 2014)
Department of the Treasury
Internal Revenue Service (99)

Request for Innocent Spouse Relief

▶ Information about Form 8857 and its separate instructions is at *www.irs.gov/form8857.*

OMB No. 1545-1596

Important things you should know

- **Do not file this form with your tax return.** See *Where To File* in the instructions.
- Review and follow the instructions to complete this form. Instructions can be obtained at *www.irs.gov/form8857* or by calling 1-800-TAX-FORM (1-800-829-3676).
- While your request is being considered, the IRS generally cannot collect any tax from you for the year(s) you request relief. However, filing this form extends the amount of time the IRS has to collect the tax you owe, if any, for those years.
- The IRS is required by law to notify the person on line 5 that you requested this relief. That person will have the opportunity to participate in the process by completing a questionnaire about the tax years you enter on line 3. This will be done before the IRS issues preliminary and final determination letters.
- The IRS will not disclose the following information: your current name, address, phone numbers, or employer.

Part I Should you file this form?

Generally, both you and your spouse are responsible, jointly and individually, for paying any tax, interest, or penalties from your joint return. If you believe your current or former spouse should be solely responsible for an erroneous item or an underpayment of tax from your joint tax return, you may be eligible for innocent spouse relief.

Innocent spouse relief may also be available if you were a resident of a community property state (see list of community property states in the instructions) and did not file a joint federal income tax return and you believe you should not be held responsible for the tax attributable to an item of community income.

1 **Do either of the paragraphs above describe your situation?**
☐ Yes. You should file this Form 8857. Go to question 2.
☐ No. Do not file this Form 8857, but go to question 2 to see if you need to file a different form.

2 **Did the IRS take your share of a joint refund from any tax year to pay any of the following past-due debt(s) owed ONLY by your spouse?** • Child support • Spousal support • Student loan (or other federal nontax debt) • Federal or state taxes
☐ Yes. You may be able to get back your share of the refund. See Form 8379, Injured Spouse Allocation, and the instructions to that form. Go to question 3 if you answered "Yes" to question 1.
☐ No. Go to question 3 if you answered "Yes" to question 1. If you answered "No" to question 1, do not file this form.

3 **If you determine you should file this form, enter each tax year you want innocent spouse relief.** It is important to enter the correct year. For example, if the IRS used your 2011 income tax refund to pay a 2009 joint tax liability, enter tax year 2009, not tax year 2011.

Tax Year		Tax Year		Tax Year	
Tax Year		Tax Year		Tax Year	

Part II Tell us about yourself and your spouse for the tax years you want relief

4 Your current name (see instructions)

	Your social security number

Address where you wish to be contacted. If this is a change of address, see instructions.

Number and street or P.O. box

Apt. no.	County

City, town or post office, state, and ZIP code. If a foreign address, see instructions.

Best or safest daytime phone number (between 6 a.m. and 5 p.m. Eastern Time)

5 **Who was your spouse for the tax years you want relief?** File a separate Form 8857 for tax years involving different spouses or former spouses.

That person's current name

	Social security number (if known)

Current home address (number and street) (if known). If a P.O. box, see instructions.

Apt. no.

City, town or post office, state, and ZIP code. If a foreign address, see instructions.

Daytime phone number (between 6 a.m. and 5 p.m. Eastern Time)

For Privacy Act and Paperwork Reduction Act Notice, see instructions.

Cat. No. 24647V

Form **8857** (Rev. 1-2014)

Note. If you need more room to write your answer for any question, attach more pages. Be sure to write your name and social security number on the top of all pages you attach.

<table>
<tr><td>**Part II**</td><td>**Tell us about yourself and your spouse for the tax years you want relief** *(Continued)*</td></tr>
</table>

6   **What is the current marital status between you and the person on line 5?**

☐ Married and still living together

☐ Married and living apart since _____
                                   MM   DD   YYYY

☐ Widowed since _____   Attach a photocopy of the death certificate and will (if one exists).
                        MM   DD   YYYY

☐ Legally separated since _____   Attach a photocopy of your entire separation agreement.
                          MM   DD   YYYY

☐ Divorced since _____   Attach a photocopy of your entire divorce decree.
                        MM   DD   YYYY

Note. A divorce decree stating that your former spouse must pay all taxes does not necessarily mean you qualify for relief.

7   **What was the highest level of education you had completed when the return(s) were filed?** If the answers are **not** the same for all tax years, explain.

☐ Did not complete high school

☐ High school diploma or equivalent

☐ Some college

☐ College degree or higher. List any degrees you have ▶ ....

List any college-level business or tax-related courses you completed ▶ ....

Explain ▶ ....

8   **Were you or other members of your family a victim of spousal abuse or domestic violence, or suffering the effects of such abuse during any of the tax years you want relief or when any of the returns were filed for those years?**

☐ Yes. If you want the IRS to consider this information in making its determination, complete Part V of this form in addition to other parts of the form. First read the instructions for Part V, to understand how the IRS will proceed with evaluating your claim for relief in these circumstances.

If you checked "Yes" above, we will put a note on your separate account. This will enable us to respond appropriately and be sensitive to your situation. We will remove the note from your account if you request it (as explained in the instructions).
If you do not want us to put a note on your account, check here . . . . ▶ ☐

☐ No. Complete the other parts of this form except for Part V.

9   **When any of the returns listed on line 3 were filed, did you have a mental or physical health problem or do you have a mental or physical health problem now?** If the answers are **not** the same for all tax years, explain below.

☐ Yes. **Attach a statement** to explain the problem and **when** it started. Provide photocopies of any documentation, such as medical bills or a doctor's report or letter.

☐ No.

Explain ▶ ....
....

10   **Is there any information you are afraid to provide on this form, but are willing to discuss?**

☐ Yes   ☐ No

<table>
<tr><td>**Part III**</td><td>**Tell us if and how you were involved with finances and preparing returns for those tax years**</td></tr>
</table>

11   **Did you agree to file a joint return?**   ☐ Yes   ☐ No

Explain why or why not ▶ ....
....
....
....
....

12   **Did you sign the joint return?** See instructions.   ☐ Yes   ☐ No

Explain why or why not ▶ ....
....
....
....

Note. If you need more room to write your answer for any question, attach more pages. Be sure to write your name and social security number on the top of all pages you attach.

Part III   Tell us if and how you were involved with finances and preparing returns for those tax years *(Continued)*

13   **What was your involvement with preparing the returns?** Check all that apply and explain, if necessary. If the answers are **not** the same for all tax years, explain.

- ☐ You were not involved in preparing the returns.
- ☐ You filled out or helped fill out the returns.
- ☐ You gathered receipts and cancelled checks.
- ☐ You gave tax documents (such as Forms W-2, 1099, etc.) for the preparation of the returns.
- ☐ You reviewed the returns before they were filed.
- ☐ You did not review the returns before they were filed. Explain below why you did not review the returns.
- ☐ You did not know a joint return was filed.
- ☐ Other ▶ ....

Explain how you were involved ▶ ....

....

14   **When the returns were filed, what did you know about any incorrect or missing information?** Check all that apply and explain, if necessary. If the answers are **not** the same for all tax years, explain below.

- ☐ You knew something was incorrect or missing, but you said nothing. Explain below.
- ☐ You knew something was incorrect or missing and asked about it. Explain below.
- ☐ You did not know anything was incorrect or missing.
- ☐ Not applicable. There was no incorrect or missing information.

Explain ▶ ....

....

15   **When any of the returns were filed, what did you know about the income of the person on line 5?** Check all that apply and explain, if necessary. If the answers are **not** the same for all tax years, explain.

- ☐ You knew that the person on line 5 had income.

    List each type of income on the lines provided below. (Examples are wages, social security, gambling winnings, or self-employment business income.) Enter each tax year and the amount of income for each type you listed. If you do not know any details, enter "I don't know."

    ....

    ....

    ....

    ....

- ☐ You knew that the person on line 5 was self-employed and you helped with the books and records.
- ☐ You knew that the person on line 5 was self-employed and you did not help with the books and records.
- ☐ You knew that the person on line 5 had no income.
- ☐ You did not know whether the person on line 5 had income.

Explain why you did not know whether the person on line 5 had income ▶ ....

16   **When the returns were filed, did you know if the returns showed a balance due to the IRS for those tax years?** If the answers are **not** the same for all tax years, explain.

- ☐ Yes. Explain when and how you thought the amount of tax reported on the return would be paid ▶ ....

    ....

    ....

- ☐ No. Explain why you did not know the return showed a balance due. ▶ ....

    ....

    ....

- ☐ Not applicable. There was no balance due on the return.

17   **When any of the returns were filed, were you having financial problems** (for example, bankruptcy or bills you could not pay)? If the answers are **not** the same for all tax years, explain.

- ☐ Yes. Explain ▶ ....

- ☐ No.
- ☐ Did not know. Explain ▶ ....

Note. If you need more room to write your answer for any question, attach more pages. Be sure to write your name and social security number on the top of all pages you attach.

Part III   Tell us if and how you were involved with finances and preparing returns for those tax years *(Continued)*

18   **For the years you want relief, how were you involved in the household finances?** Check all that apply. If the answers are **not** the same for all tax years, explain.

☐ You were not involved in handling money for the household. Explain below.

☐ You knew the person on line 5 had separate accounts.

☐ You had joint accounts with the person on line 5, but you had limited use of them or did not use them. Explain below.

☐ You used joint accounts with the person on line 5. You made deposits, paid bills, balanced the checkbook, or reviewed the monthly bank statements.

☐ You made decisions about how money was spent. For example, you paid bills or made decisions about household purchases.

☐ Other ▶ --

Explain anything else you want to tell us about your household finances ▶ --

----

----

19   **Did you (or the person on line 5) incur any large expenses, such as trips, home improvements, or private schooling, or make any large purchases, such as automobiles, appliances, or jewelry, during any of the years you want relief or any later years?**

☐ Yes. Describe (a) the types and amounts of the expenses and purchases and (b) the years they were incurred or made.

☐ No.

20   **Has the person on line 5 ever transferred assets (money or property) to you?** (Property includes real estate, stocks, bonds, or other property that you own or possess now or possessed in the past.) See instructions.

☐ Yes. List the assets, the dates they were transferred, and their fair market values on the dates transferred. If the property was secured by any debt (such as a mortgage on real estate), explain who was responsible for making payments on the debt, how much was owed on the debt at the time of transfer and whether the debt has been satisfied. Explain why the assets were transferred to you. If you no longer possess or own the assets, explain what happened with the assets.

☐ No.

Part IV   Tell us about your current financial situation

21   **Tell us about your assets.** Your assets are your money and property. Property includes real estate, motor vehicles, stocks, bonds, and other property that you own. In the table below, list the amount of cash you have on hand and in your bank accounts. Also list each item of property, the fair market value (as defined in the instructions) of each item, and the balance of any outstanding loans you used to acquire each item. Do not list any money or property you listed on line 20.

Description of Assets	Fair Market Value	Balance of Any Outstanding Loans You Used To Acquire the Asset

Form **8857** (Rev. 1-2014)

Note. If you need more room to write your answer for any question, attach more pages. Be sure to write your name and social security number on the top of all pages you attach.

Part IV	Tell us about your current financial situation *(Continued)*

22 How many people are currently in your household, including yourself?   Adults _____   Children _____

23 Tell us your current average monthly income and expenses for your entire household.

Monthly Income — If family or friends are helping to support you, include the amount of support as gifts below.	Amount
Gifts	
Wages (Gross pay)	
Pensions	
Unemployment	
Social security	
Government assistance, such as housing, food stamps, grants	
Alimony	
Child support	
Self-employment business income	
Rental income	
Interest and dividends	
Other income, such as disability payments, gambling winnings, etc. List each type below:	
Type	
Type	
Type	
Total Monthly Income	

Monthly Expenses — Enter all expenses, including expenses paid with income from gifts.	Amount
Food and Personal Care:	
Food	
Housekeeping supplies	
Clothing and clothing services	
Personal care products and services	
Transportation:	
Auto loan/lease payment, gas, insurance, licenses, parking, maintenance, etc.	
Public transportation	
Housing and Utilities:	
Rent or mortgage	
Real estate taxes and insurance	
Electric, oil, gas, water, trash, etc.	
Telephone and cell phone	
Cable and Internet	
Medical:	
Health insurance premiums	
Out-of-pocket expenses	
Other:	
Child and dependent care	
Caregiver expenses	
Income tax withholding (federal, state, and local)	
Estimated tax payments	
Term life insurance premiums	
Retirement contributions (employer required)	
Retirement contributions (voluntary)	
Union dues	
Unpaid state and local taxes (minimum payment)	
Student loans (minimum payment)	
Court-ordered debt payments (for example, court- or agency-ordered child support, alimony and garnishments). List each type below:	
Type	
Type	
Type	
Miscellaneous	
Total Monthly Expenses	

Form **8857** (Rev. 1-2014)

Note. If you need more room to write your answer for any question, attach more pages. Be sure to write your name and social security number on the top of all pages you attach.

Part V   Complete this part if you were (or are now) a victim of domestic violence or spousal abuse

As stated in line 8, providing this additional information is not mandatory but may strengthen your request. **Additionally, if you prefer to provide this information orally, check the "Yes" box on line 10.**

If you were (or are now) a victim of domestic violence or spousal abuse by the person on line 5, the IRS will consider the information you provide in this part to determine whether to grant innocent spouse relief. However, the IRS is required by law to notify the person on line 5 that you requested this relief. There are no exceptions to this rule. That person will have the opportunity to participate in the process by completing a questionnaire about the tax years you entered on line 3. This will be done before the IRS issues preliminary and final determination letters. However, the IRS is also required by law to keep all the personal identifying information (such as current names, addresses, and employment-related information) of both you and the person on line 5 confidential. This means that the IRS cannot disclose one person's information to the other person. If the IRS does not grant you relief and you choose to petition the Tax Court, your personal identifying information is available, unless you ask the Tax Court to withhold it.

The person on line 5 will receive a questionnaire about the tax years you entered on line 3. Except for your current name, address, phone numbers, and employer, this form and any attachments could be disclosed to the person on line 5. If you have any privacy concerns, see instructions.

The IRS understands and is sensitive to the effects of domestic violence and spousal abuse, and encourages victims of domestic violence to call 911 if they are in immediate danger. **If you have concerns about your safety,** please consider contacting the 24-Hour (Confidential) National Domestic Violence Hotline at 1-800-799-SAFE (7233), or 1-800-787-3224 (TTY), or 1-855-812-1001 (Video Phone Only for Deaf Callers) before you file this form.

A representative from the IRS may call you to gather more information and discuss your request. Be sure you enter your correct contact information on line 4.

24a   **During any of the tax years for which you are seeking relief or when any of the returns were filed for those years, did the person on line 5 do any of the following? Check all that apply. (Note. If this does not apply to you, skip lines 24a, b, and c, and complete lines 25 through 29.)**

- ☐ Physically harm or threaten you, your children, or other members of your family.
- ☐ Sexually abuse you, your children, or other members of your family.
- ☐ Make you afraid to disagree with him/her.
- ☐ Criticize or insult you or frequently put you down.
- ☐ Withhold money for food, clothing, or other basic needs.
- ☐ Make most or all the decisions for you, including financial decisions.
- ☐ Restrict or control who you could see or talk to or where you could go.
- ☐ Isolate you or keep you from contacting your family members and/or friends.
- ☐ Cause you to fear for your safety in any other way.
- ☐ Stalk you, your children, or other members of your family.
- ☐ Abuse alcohol or drugs.

    b   **Describe the abuse you experienced, including approximately when it began and how it may have affected you, your children, or other members of your family. Explain how this abuse affected your ability to question the reporting of items on your tax return or the payment of the tax due on your return.**

----

    c   **Attach photocopies of any documentation you have, such as:**

- Protection and/or restraining order.
- Police reports.
- Medical records.
- Doctor's report or letter.
- Injury photographs.
- A statement from someone who was aware of or witnessed the abuse or the results of the abuse (notarized if possible).
- Any other documentation you may have.

25   **Are you afraid of the person listed on line 5?**
    ☐ Yes   ☐ No

26   **Does the person listed on line 5 pose a danger to you, your children, or other members of your family?**
    ☐ Yes   ☐ No

27   **Were the police, sheriff, or other law enforcement ever called?**
    ☐ Yes   ☐ No

28   **Was the person listed on line 5 charged or arrested for abusing you, your children, or other members of your family?**
    ☐ Yes. Provide details below.

    ☐ No

29   **Have you sought help from a local domestic violence program?**
    ☐ Yes. Provide details below.

    ☐ No

Form **8857** (Rev. 1-2014)

Note. If you need more room to write your answer for any question, attach more pages. Be sure to write your name and social security number on the top of all pages you attach.

Part VI	Additional Information

30   Please provide any other information you want us to consider in determining whether it would be unfair to hold you liable for the tax.

```
------------------------------------------------------------------------------------
------------------------------------------------------------------------------------
------------------------------------------------------------------------------------
------------------------------------------------------------------------------------
------------------------------------------------------------------------------------
------------------------------------------------------------------------------------
------------------------------------------------------------------------------------
------------------------------------------------------------------------------------
------------------------------------------------------------------------------------
------------------------------------------------------------------------------------
------------------------------------------------------------------------------------
------------------------------------------------------------------------------------
------------------------------------------------------------------------------------
------------------------------------------------------------------------------------
------------------------------------------------------------------------------------
------------------------------------------------------------------------------------
------------------------------------------------------------------------------------
------------------------------------------------------------------------------------
------------------------------------------------------------------------------------
------------------------------------------------------------------------------------
------------------------------------------------------------------------------------
------------------------------------------------------------------------------------
------------------------------------------------------------------------------------
------------------------------------------------------------------------------------
------------------------------------------------------------------------------------
------------------------------------------------------------------------------------
------------------------------------------------------------------------------------
------------------------------------------------------------------------------------
------------------------------------------------------------------------------------
------------------------------------------------------------------------------------
------------------------------------------------------------------------------------
------------------------------------------------------------------------------------
```

Part VII	Tell us if you would like a refund

31   By checking this box and signing this form, you are indicating that you would like a refund if you qualify for relief and if you already paid the tax. See instructions   .   .   .   . ☐

Caution
By signing this form, you understand that, by law, we must contact the person on line 5. See instructions for details.

Sign Here
Keep a copy for your records.

Under penalties of perjury, I declare that I have examined this form and any accompanying schedules and statements, and to the best of my knowledge and belief, they are true, correct, and complete. Declaration of preparer (other than taxpayer) is based on all information of which preparer has any knowledge.

Your signature			Date

Paid Preparer Use Only	Print/Type preparer's name	Preparer's signature	Date	Check ☐ if self-employed	PTIN
	Firm's name ▶			Firm's EIN ▶	
	Firm's address ▶			Phone no.	

Form **8857** (Rev. 1-2014)

www.ingramcontent.com/pod-product-compliance
Lightning Source LLC
Chambersburg PA
CBHW072132270326
41931CB00010B/1737